A WATCHMAN'S CRY

Exposing Deceptions and Surviving the Last Days

Amber Albrecht

PAGE PUBLISHING, INC.
New York, NY

First originally published by Page Publishing, Inc. 2017

ISBN 978-1-63568-408-7 (Paperback)
ISBN 978-1-63568-409-4 (Digital)

Printed in the United States of America

Dedicated to my Lord and Savior, Jesus Christ, and the watchman that led me to Him, Evangelist Anita Fuentes.

Table of Contents

Introduction..7

Chapter 1: How Late Is the Hour? 11
Chapter 2: What Signs Does Jesus Give for the Last Days?........16
Chapter 3: What Do Other Scriptures Say
about the Last Days?................................38
Chapter 4: What Prophecy Has Been Fulfilled?.....................49
Chapter 5: What Prophecy Is in the Process of Fulfillment?.......57
Chapter 6: What Is Yet to Be Fulfilled?.........................62
Chapter 7: What Do People Need to Know
about the Tribulation?.............................73
Chapter 8: What Do People Need to Know about the
Great Tribulation?.................................81
Chapter 9: How Can Saints Be Prepared?.........................86
Chapter 10: What Responsibilities and Physical
Preparations Are Necessary? 96
Chapter 11: What and When Is the Rapture?.....................106
Chapter 12: Why Is the Body of Christ Still Here?.............121

How to Be Born Again..124
How to Be Baptized in the Holy Spirit.........................126
Bibliography..129
For More Information 143

Introduction

THERE MAY BE THOSE OUT there wondering what is going on in the world today. The earth has exploded with chaos and emotions. Explanations have been presented for some of these events and, for others, no explanation at all. Evidence will be presented in each chapter that proves exactly what is going on right now. Each chapter read will show more and more about what is going on. This book will present the hour in which this world lives in, signs of the times at hand, prophecy fulfilled already, those in the process of fulfillment, and what is yet to come to pass. It will contain facts about when the tribulation and the great tribulation will start, how to prepare, what each person's responsibilities are, and an outline of the rapture of the body of Christ. Scripture will be used to answer some questions surrounding why this is and what to do now that this knowledge has been revealed.

Where are the answers? There is one place that truly gives the answers to the questions that are currently being asked. The answers to these questions can be found in the Bible. This book explores what is going on, how it lines up with Bible prophecy, and what else is to be expected. It will delve into instructions for every person on earth, concerning how to stay safe, where to be and when, and how to prepare for the coming day when our Lord Jesus Christ returns.

The Bible clearly shows that there are certain requirements to know if these are the last days. These can be found in the prophecy that is contained in the holy book. It shows everything the people need to know. It has all the answers. It tells what, where, when, how, and who. According to the events currently happening and their chronological order, these are the last days. The hour when Jesus returns is approaching quickly. The sequence of events shows that tribulation could start any day now. This is a time of prophetic ful- fillment and will transition into a time that will be the most horrific in human history.

There will be valuable information that everyone needs to know. Knowing these things will keep many lives out of grave danger. This information helps keep people safe and determines their role in the coming days. It is vital that this world is prepared for what is coming. This material is not meant to stir fear in anyone that remains in the Lord's protection. For those that do not belong to Jesus Christ, I can say there is a good reason to be scared. No one would blame anyone that wasn't in Christ if they were scared out of their wits. There is a good reason to be.

This book walks the people through a multitude of points that urgently need to be accomplished. Some of these points cannot be ignored or delayed. A few of them are extremely helpful though people can still survive even if these aren't addressed. Know this: everyone must be prepared for the hour we live in. It could mean the difference of life and death. There will be chapters with specific instructions and scriptural references to these instructions. Following these instructions will allow anyone to be ready and fearless of what is at the door. This book is issued as a warning to all. It is a trumpet sounding in a time of trials and tribulations that can easily overcome the strongest person.

Ezekiel 33:1–5 states that the Word of the Lord came unto Ezekiel, saying when, not *if*, God brings the sword on the land. The people are to set a watchman that will blow the trumpet and sound the warning of the coming judgment. The watchman's job is to warn the people of danger in order to save them. Those that are willing to listen will be saved, and those that don't listen will not be. If someone doesn't listen to the cry of the watchman, it is their own fault, but if the watchman never cries out, then it is the watchman's fault. There is a different job for everyone in the body of Christ. This book is the cry of one that was given the job of a watchman on the wall. Who will hear the cry of this watchman sounding the trumpet in these last days?

CHAPTER 1

How Late Is the Hour?

TWO THOUSAND YEARS AGO, THE most important book ever written came to be. Its whole purpose is, was, and will be to convey God's Word to the people on this earth for thousands of years to come. It is today a collection of books, some of which are even older than two thousand years.

Over the years, there have been many that claimed the end of days was here. Some people even set dates of when they thought rapture would be. They have made claim after claim that the book of Revelation was upon the world without actually lining the events up with the chronological order of Bible prophecy. In order to assert that the end times are here, there must be a proper sequence of events.

In order to determine if this sequence of events is occurring properly, there is one reference point available. It is the only reference that can be used as it is the only one that has been issued under the proper channels. The future is only known by one entity, and that is God the Father. There are no psychics or tarot readers that can predict the end of ages. Those people are really just possessed by demonic spirits that do not predict the future but simply make the future they speak occur. The devil is a liar.

God knows exactly when everything will happen and has laid out everything His people need to know ahead of time through the prophets of old. Each of them wrote it down in their own books, and those books were gathered by God into one big book, now known as the Bible. The Bible is God's Word. It is truth, knowledge, and a manual for all that happens in life and after death. The Bible shows us precisely what to do to prepare us for the Second Coming of Christ and the tribulation.

Matthew 24 (Matt. 24:32–34, King James Version of the Holy Bible) shows that a certain event must occur before any of the rest of the signs can be taken into account. First, it states outright that it is a parable and must be understood in the comparison. To understand this parable, we refer to Romans, John, Matthew, and many others, but these will suffice for now (Rom. 11; John 15:1–8; Matt. 7:16–20).

Romans compares Israel, God's chosen people, to an olive tree. It states that Israel is the tree and that those that didn't accept Christ as the Messiah were cut out of that tree (Rom. 11). This allows the Gentiles that do accept Christ to be grafted into that tree as part of Israel, like adopted children. Gentiles that are part of the body of Christ are now referred to as Israel as well. It warns not to reject the original Jewish people because just before the end of days, they will accept Jesus and be grafted back into the tree. The main point is that Israel is a tree in this parable.

Then, when looking at John, Jesus is the true vine, and the branches are each member of the body of Christ (John 15:1–8). It is already established that these members are joined with Israel itself. Once again Jesus is speaking of cutting branches off. In this case, it is of those Christians that do not bear good fruit, and He will cast them into the fire. In other words, there is no "once saved, always saved" because a person must remain in Jesus and bear the fruit of the Spirit listed in Galatians (Gal. 5:22–23). The point once again is that Israel and the body of Christ are spoken of as a tree. Christ is the head of the body and the true vine, and the saints are the branches of this tree or vine.

In Matthew, the same comparison is used again (Matt. 7:16–20). This time Jesus even refers to gathering figs in the thistle. This passage explains how to identify an actual Christian over a person that just claims to be a Christian but doesn't truly follow Jesus. They are identified by the fruit from the tree.

As it shows, there are many comparisons to Israel and trees. By this tone, it can be safely understood that the fig tree in Matthew is

Israel itself (Matt. 24:32–34). The first verse addressed here, which the Bible communicates, is that when a tree is new and tender, it starts to put forth leaves and this is a sign that summer is near (Matt. 24:32). In other words, it is spring, the season of rebirth, and summer, the season of heat, and drought is close. When this verse is compared to the other parables, it is obvious that the rebirth of this fig tree speaks of the rebirth of Israel as a nation.

In the next verse, it goes on to say that if you recognize and see all the signs listed in the beginning of Matthew 24 after the rebirth of Israel, then you should know the end is at the door or right around the corner (Matt. 24:33).

There is even a time frame in the following verse: Matthew 24:34. It says this generation shall not pass until the end has come. So what can be derived from this? From the time the nation of Israel was reborn in 1948, the signs will increase like labor pains or birth pangs until Jesus returns. This will happen before the generation that was born in 1948 passes. This means this is the last generation. It tells the world that the hour is late and midnight is figuratively only a few minutes away.

As the chapter continues, it expresses that no one will know the hour or the day and rightly so. Just as the analogy used before, though, saints walking in the Spirit are meant to recognize the season and know when it is at the door. If the body of Christ wasn't meant to recognize and know that the last days were here, then Jesus wouldn't have said any of this. Not only did he map it out completely, but God also saw to it that it is included in the gospels three times. It isn't hidden in an inconspicuous place but repeated three times in three out of the four most read books in the Bible. Three is the number of confirmation of the Lord.

Israel has been reborn, and the signs Jesus laid out for us are behaving just as a woman's contractions. These are the end times, the last days on earth. Tribulation is just around the corner. It could literally start any day now. Now it's time to explore the instructions the Lord has for everyone. Life does come with instructions. It comes with a manual that leads God's children through every step of the way.

The Holy Bible contains instructions for everyday life as well as specific instructions prepared for certain times in the age of man. The world has entered one of those certain times. It is probably one of the most significant times there will ever be. It is only surpassed in importance by the Crucifixion and Resurrection of our Lord Jesus Christ and His Second Coming to this earth and by the Creation of this world by God Almighty. It stands equal to the flood in the days of Noah. Once again, this world has become so full of abominations in the Lord's sight it is too evil to go on this way. There remain only a couple of options.

The most favorable option falls under 2 Chronicles (2 Chron. 7:14). This verse would, of course, bring great happiness to all involved, especially God. This verse is a covenant between the Father and Israel. The whole body of Christ, Gentiles and Jews alike, are now Israel in God's eyes according to Romans (Rom. 11).

It states: "If my people, which are called by my name, shall humble themselves, and pray, and seek my face, and turn away from their wicked ways; then I will hear from heaven, and will forgive their sin, and will heal their land" (2 Chron. 7:14).

This would call for the majority of the world to fall on their face in repentance and renounce all false gods and idols (including money, video games, fame, celebrities, etc.) and to turn to God and follow His commandments. Abortion would be made illegal globally. Traditional marriage would be the only legal and accepted form of marriage. Sin would be called sin and be rebuked, not tolerated and understood. Instead of being politically correct, the world would worry about being biblically correct.

Fornication wouldn't be accepted just because of the need to "get with the times." Sex outside of marriage, including living together, wouldn't be accepted. Divorce rates would drop by 80 percent or more because Jesus doesn't approve of divorce except in the situation of fornication and not to mention divorce usually leads to adultery. Matthew states that Jesus says those that remarry after a divorce, other than for the reason of fornication (adultery), are committing adultery themselves because they are with someone other than their original spouse. A granted divorce only frees one to leave and be alone, not remarry unless fornication was involved. Ultimately, the world would bow to Jesus, and we would finally be rid of most evil.

This is on most Christians' prayer list on a daily basis. God is a gentleman, however, and will not go where He is not welcome. He gave every person free will. He doesn't want weekend visitations on Sunday and Wednesday nights. God wants full custody. Therefore, the likelihood of this happening on a global scale is slim. Islam, Hindu, New Age, and all other religions would become almost non-existent at the level needed to wipe the abominations off the face of the earth. Anything is possible through Christ, who strengthens us, so it will continue to be on many prayer lists everywhere.

The second option is this. God is fed up with the abominations before His eyes. He is compelled by the innocent blood of the saints being persecuted and unborn babies crying out from the ground. We learn this from Proverbs and other verses (Prov. 6:16–19). When the world reaches this point and God has been as long-suffering as He can be, after choosing the perfect time to assure as many as possible are saved, He will bring judgment on the rest of the earth. Just as He did in the days of Noah, the wicked will be punished, and the righteous, who have received Jesus, will be protected from all but persecution. This scenario ends in the Second Coming of Jesus Christ to defeat the Antichrist in the battle of Armageddon after a seven-year period known as the tribulation and great tribulation.

CHAPTER 2

What Signs Does Jesus Give for the Last Days?

IN THIS SCENARIO, GOD HAS explained everything a person needs to know about the whole end-time situation in Bible prophecy. Matthew, Mark, and Luke are all very similar (Matt. 24; Mark 13; Luke 21). They are three different accounts by an apostle of Jesus Himself and others in the early church, teaching what the sign of this time will be. It is not only the teachings of Jesus Christ Himself but also specific warnings and basically a map for us to correctly identify that time period.

Obviously, the first thing He said was a prophecy that has already been fulfilled in AD 70 when the second temple was destroyed. Matthew shows the disciples asking Jesus for the signs of His Second Coming and the end of the world (Matt. 24:3). The very next thing out of Jesus's mouth is a warning. In Matthew alone, there are six warnings for us not to be deceived by false prophets and men saying they are Christ (Matt. 24).

He states that many will be deceived by these men. It is noticeable in the Bible that when God wants something to be understood and not missed, it is repeated over and over again. There is also the use of the phrase "He who hath ears let him hear." This whole chapter is unmistakably very important as it is repeated in Matthew, Mark, and Luke (Matt. 24; Mark 13; Luke 21).

There are many that have come to this earth, claiming to be Christ, and all of them cannot be addressed here. Here are a few of the more famous situations and also a few of the most recent.

Bernhard Muller was also known as Count de Leon. He was born in Germany in 1788. He claimed in 1829 to be the Lion of Judah and a prophet that had the philosopher's stone, which was a substance they felt would make alchemy a success. He eventually died after fleeing Pennsylvania to Ohio and then to Louisiana when he contracted yellow fever or cholera (quoted in Wikipedia, Bautz and Traugott, Bd. 23; Conrad, "Leon, Count").

There was Arnold Potter. He was a Latter-Day Saint schismatic leader and referred to himself as the Potter Christ. He was born in New York in 1804 and moved to Illinois in 1840. He received a blessing from Joseph Smith himself, who is another false prophet, and was ordained to priesthood of the elder. Brigham Young sent him from San Bernardino, California, to Australia on a mission trip in 1856, during which Potter says Christ entered his body and he became Potter Christ, Son of the Living God (Potter, "Revelations of Potter Christ"; Rich, *Those Who Would*).

Of course, there is the famous Charles Manson, who was born in 1934. He believed he was the Second Coming of Christ, and allegedly, to punish the Jewish people that didn't believe in him, he carved a swastika on his head. In an attempt to start an apocalyptic race war, which he called Helter Skelter, his "family" committed several horrific murders in 1969 (Bugliosi and Gentry, *Helter Skelter)*

Jose Luis de Jesus Miranda makes a double claim. He claims the Antichrist just means the Second Coming of Christ. He says he is both. He says there is no such thing as sin except for one. The world must give him money. His followers have faithfully had 666 tattooed on their body, including one mother putting the mark on her three-year-old son, in the movement that started in Miami, Florida. He was born in Puerto Rico in 1946. He said he was visited by angels in 1973 and that the spirit that was in Jesus of Nazareth entered him at that moment. His followers even celebrated Christmas on April 22, his birthday (Avila, "Jesus of Suburbia"; "Crowd Packs Amphitheater";

" Miami-based 'Antichrist'"; "Mother Tattoos Religious"; Malisow, "Jesus Christ Celebrates").

Another famous person to assert that they were Christ was Jim Jones, born in 1931 in Indiana. He was a communist that worked for civil rights, but this quickly turned into something sinister. He became a reverend and launched his own church, which became the People's Temple.

His message that he called the gospels was actually of communism and socialism. He preached that a person born into capitalism was born in sin and someone born into socialism wasn't born into sin. He taught that traditional Christianity was a fly-away religion and that the Bible was just a tool to suppress women and nonwhites, and he denounced what he called the Sky God. He then claimed he was the reincarnation of Mahatma Gandhi, Father Divine, Jesus, Buddha, and Lenin. Hue Fortson Jr., a former Temple member, quoted Jones as saying, "What you need to believe in is what you can see. ... If you see me as your friend, I'll be your friend. If you see me as your father, I'll be your father, for those of you that don't have a father. ... If you see me as your savior, I'll be your savior. If you see me as your god, I'll be your god." Jones, his family, and several hundred Temple members moved their compound to Guyana after many moves across the United States and Brazil. He named the settlement Jonestown, where no one was permitted to leave ever. It was here where Jones attained his belief in translation, where he and his followers would die together and move to another planet. He poisoned the whole community with cyanide, killing 909 people, of which 304 were children (Wessinger, p. 200; *Jonestown: The Life and Death*).

David Koresh—or Vernon Wayne Howell, as he was born in 1959—was the leader of the Branch Davidians and was a Seventh-Day Adventist. In 1983, he claimed the gift of prophecy, and in 1985, he claimed he was a modern-day Cyrus while setting up a camp in Palestine, Texas. He believed he would set up the Davidic kingdom in Jerusalem until 1990 but in 1991 declared it was to be in the United States. He claimed the prophecies of Daniel would be fulfilled in Waco. In 1990 he had his name changed to David Koresh—

Koresh being the Persian name of Cyrus the great, and David being King David. After his claims that he was a descendant of King David and a messianic figure on a divine errand, his compound was finally raided in 1993 by ATF over child abuse charges. This resulted in ten deaths in the initial raid when the FBI took over. After a fifty-one-day standoff, the Branch Davidians set the place on fire, and all eighty inside died ("Waco: The Inside Story"; Pitts, "Davidians and Branch Davidians").

Then there is Alan John Miller, who started a group called Divine Truth in 2005. He says he is Jesus of Nazareth through reincarnation and is an elder in the Jehovah's Witnesses. His partner, Mary Suzanne Luck, claims to be the reincarnation of Mary Magdalene. He says he has memories of being Jesus since he was two and can't perform miracles yet because he isn't at that stage in this life yet ("Messiah Complex"; Murray, "Jesus and Mary Cult"; "Man Claims to be Jesus").

The next sign listed is wars and rumors of wars. There has always been war and conflicts on this earth, but it wasn't until the twentieth century that world wars arose. The wars have been getting bloodier, more severe, more widespread, and more frequent consistently. Again listing all the information wouldn't be a possible. No one wants to read thirty chapters just listing dates and conflicts. In no certain order, there are many that will be mentioned.

The most notable ongoing war at the moment is the war on terror. At this time, the world is fervently trying to subdue one of the most brutal terror organizations we can think of. ISIS has virtually thrown the Middle East into mayhem single-handedly. There are two different coalitions currently formed to combat ISIS in Syria and Iraq. This war has spread to many places in the form of terror attacks either by ISIS or inspired by them, such as those in France, Belgium, United States, Turkey, Australia, Yemen, a Russian plane in Egypt, Algeria, Canada, Saudi Arabia, Libya, Bosnia and Herzegovina, Lebanon, Denmark, Tunisia, Afghanistan, Kuwait, Germany, Bangladesh, and Indonesia.

Then there are the other Islamic jihadist groups and terror organizations included in the war on terror, such as al-Qaeda,

Boko Haram, Hamas, Hezbollah, ANO, ASG, AUM, Islamic Group, HUM, Kach, LTTE, National Liberation Army, Palestine Liberation Front, Palestinian Islamic Jihad, PFLF, Islamic Movement of Uzbekistan, and a lot more (US Dept. of State, "Foreign Terrorist Organization").

Then there are also regular conflicts and wars / proxy wars, some of which never really seem to end. Currently, Israel is under constant terror attacks from Palestinians with the threat of the start of a third intifada. In 2014 Operation Protective Edge was considered an intifada, which consisted of war between Gaza and Israel. It left Gaza devastated after they attacked Israel, and Israel responded with blunt defensive force. That is Bible prophecy in itself in another manner according to Zephaniah (Zeph. 2:4).

There is the Yemeni Crisis, which started in 2011 and has now become the Yemen Civil War. In actuality, it is a proxy war between the Saudi Arabian–backed Yemeni government and the Iranian–backed Houthi rebels. Basically, Saudi Arabia and Iran are at war, using their own pawns to carry it out. This isn't the only proxy war going on right now. Russia and the United States are in a proxy war, using Syria as a cover. Russia backs Bashar al-Assad, the Syrian regime president, and the United States is currently funding moderate rebels and providing them with all manner of weaponry and supplies, which ISIS conveniently keeps getting their hands on. This is known as the Syrian Civil War.

The Libyan Civil War is a hot topic in America right now after Hillary Clinton "allegedly" was a part in letting Americans die with stand-down orders while the embassy was being overrun and lying to the families about what caused the situation. It has been going on since 2011 and before really, but that is its documented date. Things really started to escalate when the Arab Spring was inspired, some say by President Obama, and spread from Libya to Egypt and Tunisia. This caused riots in the streets of Egypt in 2013 (Rubin, *NY Times*: "Obama Jump-Started").

There are countless more, such as the war in Afghanistan, the Iraq War, the Kurdish/Turkish Conflict in 1984 (which led to the PKK Rebellion in 2015), the Somalia Civil War, and the war in northwest Pakistan in 2004, the Mexican Drug War of 2006, and the Sinai insurgency in 2011. There were wars in the Central African Republic and northern Mali in 2012, all of which have been in the news. Don't forget this whole business with Russia and Ukraine that Putin insists isn't happening. There is Nigeria, Sudan, Uganda, and many more. Then there are the looming threats of World War 3 trying to start around every corner, which could lead us to the first Gog and Magog war from Ezekiel 38 (this will be discussed more at length later on). North Korea, China, Iran, and Russia are threatening the United States with war or nuclear war every time they turn a corner. Iran and Turkey just can't resist threatening Israel's very existence. Russia is showing muscle and signs of moving against NATO countries, and round and round it goes.

This contributes to the verse in which it speaks of nation against nation, kingdom against kingdom. As Matthew moves on, it lists more signs that become undeniable as to the hour this world is in (Matt. 24:7–8). The verses that coincide in Mark and Luke even add more detail to the list (Mark 13; Luke 21). There shall be famines, pestilence, earthquakes in diverse (*divers*, as written in the Bible) places, fearful sights, and great signs. It describes these things as the beginning of sorrows. In *Strong's Concordance,* sorrows is defined as a pang or throe, especially of childbirth—pain, sorrow, travail (Thayer and Smith, #5604 entry for *odin*). This would mean that these signs will increase in intensity and frequency right up until the return of Christ. Just as a woman's labor contractions, they come, subside, and come back a little stronger and a little more often with each round.

First, there is the breakdown of some of the famines across the globe. Record-breaking droughts and food shortages are hitting in multiple places. Canada, California, Washington State, Oregon, and parts of Texas in 2015 have seen unthinkable drought that have caused uncontrollable wildfires, water restrictions, and the use of almost all the stored groundwater in these areas.

East Africa was hit very hard beginning in 2011, killing 260,000 people in Somalia alone, and China suffered horribly, starting in 2008 (AP, "Famine Toll"; *U.S.D.A. Foreign Agricultural Service Commodity Report; UN News Centre, "U.N. Declares Famine"*). Along with China, 2008 brought massive droughts that led to loss of crops and many deaths across Argentina, Brazil, Paraguay, Uruguay, Chile, and Afghanistan, and that didn't all just hold to that year (Price, "Argentine Drought"; Wheeland," Brazil Struggles"; CIA, World Fact Book; Gedan, "Uruguay Drought"; Martinez and Yulkowski, "Chile Government Hands Out Water"; Budde, Rowland and Verdin *Assessing the Impacts*). Brazil is devastated as the drought is even worse now. In 2009 Iraq, Israel, Lebanon, Bangladesh, and Myanmar joined these countries. India, Tajikistan, Turkmenistan, Thailand, Nepal, Pakistan, and Turkey saw drought as well in 2009 to the extent that food production was cut by 20 to 40 percent (AP, "Iraq Drought Hits Marshes"; JP, "Drought and the Treasury"; Gallart, "Drought and Misuse"; UN General Assembly, ReliefWeb, "International Cooperation"; "Asia Pacific Food"; "Countries Affected By Global Food Crisis"; USDA, *Middle East and Central Asia;"*; Siegel-Itzkovich, *"NASA Finds"*). In 2007 Bolivia, the Horn of Africa, and Jordan were in a severe drought.

The drought in Europe in 2003 killed 23,700 people. North Korea saw record deaths in the shortages of 1996. Different sources have varying numbers for death tolls in a range from 200,000 up to 3,500,000 people (French Heat Toll"; "Drought in Cochabamba"; *Encyclopedia Britannica*, "North Korea 1996"; "North Korea Pledged Aid"; Lankov, "N Korea and the Myth"; O. Grada, p. 24; USDA, "Middle East: Deficient Rainfall"). Seventy thousand died from heat and lack of water in Sudan in 1998.

From 1998 to 2004, the second Congo War raged on (HSRP, "Death Toll"). Most lost their lives not by conflict but from starvation and disease from the drought and lack of food due to the war. The cost was 3,800,000 people. The conditions in Somalia in 1991 and 1992 due to lack of water killed three hundred thousand people (Spagat, Mack, Cooper, and Kreutz, "Estimating War Deaths"). There are many more instances, and they keep getting worse. The news reported today that a city in Alberta, Canada, is being evacuated completely due to the inability to stop the wildfire in the area after a few years of bad drought and the winds ("Devastating Wildfire").

There is no way to list every single instance of pestilence. There are two different forms of pestilence. One can consider the diseases and the infestations of actual pests. To address the diseases, there is a reference to the WHO outbreak list from 2010 to April 2016, omitting locations as it makes it far more extensive. Some of these are listed as epidemics and some pandemics. Others are simply listed as outbreaks. There has been ebola, legionnaires' disease, the measles, Zika virus, and West Nile virus (both carried by the pestilence of mosquitos). The plague has taken several lives here in the US, originating from Yosemite and Yellowstone National Parks from another pestilence, fleas. There is an AIDS epidemic again. MERS (Middle East respiratory syndrome), Lassa fever, bird flu (human cases as well), yellow fever, cholera, *Elizabethkingia*, microcephaly, Guillian-Barre syndrome, dengue fever, and chikungunya are out with a vengeance.

Polio is back! Meningococcal disease, typhoid fever, Marburg virus, wild poliovirus and poliovirus, novel coronavirus, Marburg hemorrhagic fever, rift valley fever, and hantavirus pulmonary syndrome have swept through different countries. Hand-foot-and-mouth-disease seems to be a rather big problem. There are three undiagnosed illnesses in Cambodia. They have no idea and couldn't tell the WHO what they are. There are influenzalike illnesses listed as well as poliomyelitis, EHEC, hemolytic uremic syndrome, and Crimean-Congo hemorrhagic fever. H1N1, more commonly known as swine flu, gave everyone quite a scare and was labeled as a pandemic. The list goes on, but there just isn't enough time or paper. Quite frankly, if someone had to read that many news stories and lists of diseases with full information, they would probably fall asleep (WHO PEP, "WHO Disease Outbreaks by Year").

Next addressed is another form of pestilence. There are the fleas at Yellowstone and Yosemite National Park, causing the plague, and the mosquitos across the southern portion of the United States and Caribbean, stretching down to South America (Bakalar, "Plague Cases"; News Release, "Bubonic Plague Diagnosed"; US Dept. of Interior NPS, "Plague in Yosemite"). There have been countless outbreaks of rats, mice, locusts, bed bugs, termites, beetles, flies (yes, like the plagues of Egypt), scorpions, worms, maggots, killer bees, and many other varieties of diseases carrying vermin.

Here are just a few instances. They are in no particular order. In Madagascar in 2012–2013, they saw record-breaking amounts of locusts that infested 50 percent of the country. The authorities declared the situation of plague status. Eyewitnesses stated that you couldn't see anything but locusts everywhere. News of the infestation went global just before Passover, and it was compared with the biblical plagues of Egypt. It even prompted the United Nations to step in and call for donations for a proposed plan that cost forty-one million dollars. The FAO reported that it threatened 60 percent of the country's rice crop as well as livestock pastures. Officials warn that in an area already in horrible famine, the infestation could last five to ten years if left unchecked and two-thirds of Madagascar would be infected, leading to the need for massive food aid (Foley, "Biblical Locust Plague"; Hill, "Severe Locust Plague"; "Madagascar Hit by 'Severe' Plague"; Shwayder, "Locusts in Madagascar").

Locust didn't just single out Madagascar but invaded Russia as well. Swarms of locusts began at the end of July in 2015, swarming southern Russia from Chechnya to the Astrakhan Province on the Caspian Sea. A state of emergency was declared in three regions (Chance, "Locust Swarms Plague"; Reevell, "Video: Plague of Locust"). They also descended on Herald, California, and ABC News reported it as a swarm of biblical proportions and called it a plague straight out of the Bible in 2012 (Rosenbaum, "Plague of Locusts"). The swarms of locusts—or, as they are called in Texas, grasshoppers—were so bad in New Mexico, Texas, and Oklahoma that they interfered with the weather radar in 2014 and 2015 (Sharpe, "Bug Swarm So Big"; Lee, "Grasshopper Outbreak Surfaces"; Jensen, "NWS Radar"). In 2016, Argentina's agriculture was threatened with devastation as an area the size of Delaware was covered in northern Argentina according to the Weather Channel. Experts say that Argentina is in it for the long haul (Crugnale, "Locusts Threaten to Devastate"). Amir Ayali, who is a professor of zoology at Tel Aviv University, was a consultant during the locust outbreak in Israel in 2013. This overrun was also just before Passover and darkened the skies as they came from Egypt. Isn't that interesting? ("Locusts Swarm Israel").

In Florida in 2013, they shut down schools over bedbugs, termites, and rat epidemics. In addition, Florida was also infested with pythons and lionfish in 2013 (AP, "Termites Strike"; Liston, "Florida Battles Slimy"; "Overwhelmed by Python"; Fleshler, "Invasive Lion Fish"). They also were or are battling giant snails, fleas, and sharks (Klaus, "Flea Infestation Invades"; Molstad, "Shark Infestation"; Santos, "Lured by Early Warm Weather"). Texas and Arizona saw many violent attacks from swarms of killer bees that infiltrated neighborhoods in 2013–2015. This came after Oklahoma had the same problem in 2012 (Johnson, "'Killer Bees' Leave Texas Man"; Mazza, "Deadly Bee Attack"; "Killer Bees Swarming"). New York, New Jersey, Connecticut, and other places in New England have had unnatural amounts of bedbugs that they can't seem to stop. The bugs are leaving sores on many residents, which just resemble the memory of another plague of Egypt ("Bed Bugs! 15 Worst Cities"; Entomological Society of America, "Study Examines Bed Bug"; Maxfield, "Bed Bug Infestation"; Siff, "'Getting' Buggy").

South Edmonton in Alberta, Canada, is battling an infestation of boring wood beetles and mountain pine beetles, which are killing 30 to 70 percent of the trees in local forests. It has also reached British Columbia and the United States (Rosner, "Bug That Is Eating the Woods"; CBC News, "Pine Beetles Continue"; Canadian Press, "Pine Beetles Find New Home"; Canadian Press, "Pine Beetles Defying"). This is no doubt in combination with the drought fueling the wildfire that caused the evacuation of eighty thousand people just yesterday on May 3, 2016. Also in 2015, the Nevada Desert encountered a battle with stink bugs (Mohney, "Nevada Burning Man Festival"). Then last but not least, there is the scorpion overrun of 2016 in Arizona (Santos, "Lured by Early Warm Weather"). There is no end to the pestilence in the form of infestations, but this will do for now.

The next sign of the end of days to mention is earthquakes in diverse places. Now this could be a big surprise to those that haven't made this connection already. There are some that have told themselves that science just detects them better. There are some that would argue other reasons, but in fact, earthquakes have most definitely been increasing in frequency and intensity, and even the scientists admit it. Geologists are doing studies, trying to explain it, and in most cases, they can't. Now remember, the Bible doesn't say that if it can be explained, then it's not God.

I know many are aware of the big earthquake in Nepal last year and the ones recently in Japan and Ecuador and so on. There are so many more that people aren't aware of. This is one of those topics that simply can't be approached by giving lists of earthquakes that are happening daily around the world. Even a list of one day's activity would be overwhelming and tedious to view. So this is going to be approached a little differently. The scientific world is jumping about the issue, so starting there sounds like a good idea.

Deanna Conners states that large earthquakes greater than 8.0 in magnitude have struck the earth at a record rate since 2004 ("Are Large Earthquakes Increasing"). They claim it is mere chance, but they offer no scientific evidence to this reasoning of randomness. They also mention earthquakes of this magnitude typically occur at a rate of one per year. In 2004 the USGS recorded two above this magnitude and two again in 2006. In 2007 they recorded four earthquakes greater than 8.0 on the Richter scale. That is quadruple the average.

Now here's a kicker. Their records indicate that a disproportionately high number of large earthquakes greater than 8.0 occurred between 1950 and 1965. That time period starts two years after the rebirth of Israel and ends two years before the biblical year of Jubilee, when Israel regained control and possession of Jerusalem during the Six-Day War (Cahn, *The Mystery of the Shemitah*; History. com staff, "Six Day War Ends"). There is more information about the year of jubilee and year of the *shemitah* available. Conners says, "Furthermore, the scientists could find no plausible physical mechanism that could explain the possible occurrence of global swarms." Even in Texas, the risk levels have been increased (Buchele, "USGS to Increase Earthquake Risk"). Well, the explanation is in Matthew, Mark, and Luke (Matt. 24; Mark 13; Luke 21).

An article by Becky Oskin states that a new study finds that there were more than twice as many big earthquakes in the first quarter of 2014 as compared with the average since 1979. Tom Parsons was the lead study author and a research geophysicist with the US Geological Survey in Menlo Park, California. He said, "We have experienced a period that has had one of the highest rates of great earthquakes ever recorded." This study again rationalizes the whole thing with random chance. Since when could random chance be proven? According to Oskin, the average rate of big earthquakes, which they define as 7.0 or larger, have been ten a year since 1979, their study reports. That rate has climbed to an average of twelve and a half per year, beginning in 1992, and then in 2010, it hiked up to 16.7 per year. That is a 65 percent increase compared to the rate in 1979 (Oskin, "Big Earthquakes Double").

The R. Lin II reported that, after a long stretch of quiet, they experienced five quakes greater than 4.0 in the last five months from the date of the article. They noted that it hadn't occurred since 1994 during the Northridge quake and its fifty-three aftershocks. Lin II also mentioned fifteen smaller earthquakes between January and March in the Santa Monica Mountains that ranged from 1.0 to 2.5, which shows seismic activity increasing under the Santa Monica Mountains. The paper reports the USGS studying an increase in quakes in central and the eastern United States in recent years larger than 3.0. They marked one hundred earthquakes per year on average for the previous four years, which is quite a rise from twenty per year between 1970 and 2000 (Lin II, "Quakes Are Increasing, but Scientists Aren't Sure").

According to USGS, the record of earthquakes supports the articles and an increase in earthquakes gradually. This was copied straight from their page:

> According to long-term records (since about 1900), we expect about 16 major earthquakes in any given year, which includes 15 earthquakes in the magnitude 7 range and one earthquake magnitude 8.0 or greater. In the past 38 years, from 1973 through 2011, our records show that

we have exceeded the long-term average number of major earthquakes only 8 times, in 1976,
1990, 1995, 1999, 2007, 2009, 2010, and 2011.
(USGS FAQs, "Why Are We Having So Many")

NBC News reports a worldwide surge in "great" earthquakes
from 2004 to 2014. "The annual number of 'great' earthquakes nearly
tripled over the last decade, providing a reminder to Americans that
unruptured faults like those in the northwest United States might
be due for a Big One," they said in an article published in October
of 2014. NBC claims an increase of 265 percent over the average
rate of the century before (Carroll, "Worldwide Surge in 'Great'
Earthquakes").

By looking at the data provided, it isn't just conspiracy theo-
rist and Bible prophecy enthusiast that have noticed the increase in
earthquakes. The Bible clearly explains the why that so many scien-
tist just can't seem to put their fingers on, minus the random excuse
or fracking fallback.

This leads to the sign of the times; those that follow Jesus will be
persecuted. They (we) will be hated because they love Him. Matthew
states that many will be offended and betray and hate one another
(Matt. 24). Mark adds more detail to the issue, saying they will deliver
Christians up to the councils or courts and the saints will be beaten
in synagogues and churches. Brothers and sisters in Christ will also
be brought before rulers and kings because of their faith in Jesus so
that they may testify and preach the gospels to the rulers of the day.
Jesus warns not to think ahead about what you will say because the
Holy Spirit will speak for you at that moment (Mark 13). Luke adds
that the body of Christ will be thrown in prisons and be betrayed by
brothers, parents, kinsfolk, and friends (Luke 21). There is already
strong evidence of persecution throughout the world on a massive
scale. It has even reached the United States in forms.

Kim Davis sat in jail for staying true to Jesus after refusing to
sign a marriage license for homosexual couples. Crosses are being torn
down all over China as Christians fight the good fight by peacefully
returning them to their place. Some are being detained and ques-
tioned for long hours. A church in Wuxi has had its water and elec-

tricity disconnected, and the government has tried to place cameras up and threatened the jobs and education of the church's members. One city, Wenzhou, known as the Jerusalem of the East, is home to a church named Sanjiang; the government of China has claimed is illegally built and will be demolished. Thousands of Christians in that city are mounting an around-the-clock human shield to protect it from the bulldozers (AP, "Chinese Christians Fight Back"; Phillips, "Christians Form Human Shield").

Meanwhile, in the Middle East, Christians are being beheaded, raped, sold as slaves, or forced to flee. Israel has labeled it genocide of Christians and urges countries in the West to recognize that fact. Religious leaders are warning the same thing. ISIS has beheaded twenty-one Coptic Christians in Egypt, captured priests, killed missionaries, and beheaded toddlers for saying, "I love Jesus." It is all over the news and everywhere you look. It is the worst persecution seen in the last twenty years (Bowcott and Jones, "Religious Leaders Say Isis Persecution"; Edwards, "You Are a Target").

North Korea just sentenced one Christian missionary to ten years of hard labor by accusing him of stealing information and passing it to South Korea. Of course, they said there was a confession, but isn't that always the story in North Korea? Human rights groups estimate there are around two hundred thousand or more in prison in North Korea for having different religious or political views than those of its leader. North Korea is ranked number one in Christian persecution. According to *USA Today*, "Anyone discovered engaging in secret religious activity may be subject to arrest, disappearance, torture, and even public execution." (Curry, "North Korea Really Isn't Funny"; Gledhill, "Christian Missionary Sentenced").

In Saudi Arabia and many other Muslim countries, it is illegal to be a Christian or speak about such things. In 2014 in Saudi Arabia, twenty-eight people were arrested in Khafji at a prayer meeting. Several Bibles were confiscated after the authorities got a tip about a home-based church. According to Fox News, Saudi Arabia's Islamic religious police continue to expunge any trace of Christianity within its territory (Weinthall, "World-Saudi Anti-Christian Sweep").

In Egypt, Coptic Christians are specifically targeted. Over forty Christian churches all over Egypt were looted and set on fire by Muslim mobs. Some of these churches were over a thousand years old. In 2015, a Muslim mob visited the homes of five Coptic Christian students in the village of Nasreya. The mob chanted the students had insulted Islam in a video showing the youths praying with their teacher. The students had been making fun of ISIS, and their teacher was arrested and kept for four days for questioning.

The mobs threw rocks at the homes, trying to scare their parents into turning them over to the authorities. Authorities use one law they have against blasphemy to persecute minorities, including Christians. The children and other victims of Muslim assaults remained in the authorities' custody. The victims usually get charged with inciting violence even though they were attacked.

Another village, called al Our, was home to thirteen out of the twenty-one Coptic Christians beheaded by ISIS in February of 2015. It was attacked by a Muslim mob that opposed the Christians' plan to build a new church in honor of the twenty-one killed by pelting them with rocks and chanting as to how they would never allow the construction to begin. President Sisi had already given permission for the church, but as soon as the customary reconciliation session was done, the Coptics were informed they must build the church outside of the village. In Maghagha City, on Good Friday, police raided an Orthodox prayer house and confiscated altar artifacts on the grounds that the worshippers were praying without permission. It also vandalized the contents of the building and took vessels used for rites (Bowcott and Jones, "Religious Leaders Say Isis Persecution"; Edwards, "You Are a Target"). The list goes on and on. Round and round she goes, and where she stops nobody knows.

A very important issue that cannot be left out is the persecution of Christians in the United States military. Two California chaplains are suing the VA for being forced out of their training and placement program because they are Christians. Chaplains Major Steven Firtko and Lieutenant Commander Dan Klender were repeatedly harassed and threatened while enrolled in San Diego Clinical Pastoral Education Center according to *Christian News*. The article reports that their supervisor and the VA "do not allow chaplains to pray in Jesus's name in public ceremonies" and that they were reprimanded for attempting to quote scripture in class on multiple occasions. The class was told God could be a man or a woman by the supervisor, and she hit the table with a fist when Firtko said the Lord's Prayer (Clark, "Military Chaplains Sue after Being Ordered").

Then there is the marine that has been court-martialed for her refusal to remove the scripture "No weapon formed against me shall prosper" from her desk, citing her religious freedom (Starnes, "Marine Court-Martialed"). A navy chaplain could see the end of a nineteen-year career because of his faith. His stance on marriage and sexuality contribute, and he was told by his base commander to refrain from praying in the name of Jesus. He is dealing with this because a homosexual officer was offended by the fact that it is a sin and has accused the chaplain of discrimination among other things. He has been dismissed from duties (Starnes, "Navy Chaplain Censored").

There is a list from Michael Snyder discussing what President Obama's definition of what an extremist is. You might be an extremist if you are any of the following:

- Anyone that possesses "intolerance for other religions," "antigay," "anti-immigrant," anti-Muslim"
- "Opposition to equal rights for gays and lesbians"
- Members of American Family Association
- Members of the Christian Action Network
- Anyone that is "opposed to the New World Order"
- Anyone opposed to Agenda 21
- Anyone concerned about FEMA camps
- Anyone that "fears impending gun control or weapons confiscations"
- Citizens that have "bumper stickers" that are patriotic or anti-UN
- Anyone that is "antiabortion"
- Those that "believe in the right to bear arms"
- Those that believe in "end time" prophecies, and evangelical Christians

Now this list contains seventy-two items, but these are a few of them. President Obama has stated these people need to be on a terror watch list according to Michael Snyder, and he cites references as well. Then they continue to say that alarms should go off when President Obama says these things and then adds he wants to crack down on extremism. In other words, the government wants to crack down on evangelical Christians that call sin what it is and believe in what the Bible says, including prophecy (Snyder, "Obama Declares War on Extremism").

There are so many more instances, but it is time to move on to the next point. Many false prophets shall arise. Now this is different from the false Christs. Here, Jesus speaks of the wolves in sheep's clothing, the preachers, pastors, professing Christians, false religions, and everyone else trying to feed the people false doctrine. The doctrine of men is not to be followed, but instead we should rebuke it and expose it. The Bible is meant to be taken for the truth that it is. It is not to be taken out of context or twisted to make it mean what people want it to mean. There is no picking out single verses and pretending they mean differently from what they would say when looked at in the whole chapter or even book.

For example, Matthew 7 is used a lot to say, "Do not judge," but in actuality, when the whole chapter is read, it says that a person shouldn't judge someone until they have first learned to live for Jesus and their life is in order, then that person can judge righteously and not by appearances. So yet another warning is given for us to not be deceived by false prophets.

There are a lot of famous ministers out there, preaching many different doctrines. Everything should be judged by scripture and taken to the Holy Spirit. There are those that have said you don't go to church for God; you go to church for you so you can be happy, and God wants us to be happy. That's a lie from the pit. The whole reason for the church is to worship and glorify the Lord and to learn how He wants His children to live. Our whole existence is to be used exalting God. Read Isaiah 25:1 and Psalm 150:6.

Some have said if you can perceive it, you can be it or have it. You are your own "I Am." Just visualize what you want and focus on it. Well, the Bible says otherwise. A Christian's goal is not supposed to be to attain their heart's desires, luxuries, or money. The goal isn't to build up treasures here on earth according to Matthew (Matt. 6:19–21). The job of a saint is to build their treasure in heaven by only wanting God's will for their lives and sharing the gospel. God's will is not for one person to gain all this wealth and material things; his will is for people to use that to feed the hungry and clothe the poor. If the preacher has a ten-million-dollar home or more, he/she is probably a false prophet. Matthew says it is easier for a camel to go through the eye of a needle than for a rich man to make it into heaven (Matt. 19:24).

Still, others are asking you for sixty-five million dollars for a jet that they must have to preach the gospel. How many children would that much money feed? How many Bibles would it buy? Now ministries do need donations to operate but not such a large amount, for things could be done in a way that wouldn't require so much funds. Please don't be deceived by people like this. One false prophet has been quoted as saying, "God sees us as a strong, successful, overcoming person." Wrong again because there is no one good but God. Every person that walks this earth is nothing without God, and He knows it and commands His children to be humble and not full of pride. It is Jesus that makes each born-again Christian whole. Without Jesus, everyone is just a broken sinner headed for the penalty of that sin, which is death.

> For all have sinned and come short of the glory of God (Rom. 3:23)

> But we are all as an unclean thing, and all our righteousnesses are as filthy rags. (Isa. 64:6)

There are those that would tell everyone they aren't saved unless they call Christ Yashua. That is just Jesus in Hebrew, and God speaks every language. There are those that claim once someone is saved, they can do anything they want because they are under grace and will be forgiven. I have even heard a preacher say (the same one that wanted the jet) that everyone has to have something to be forgiven for on Sunday. What! That is crazy talk. Matthew says don't be a wicked and lazy servant (Matt. 25:14–30). James shows that saints must be a doer of the word, not just a hearer only (James 1:19–25). Faith without works is dead according to James (James 2:17–18).

> For if we sin willfully after we have received the knowledge of truth, there remaineth no more sacrifice for our sins. (Heb. 10:26)

> What shall we say then? Shall we continue in sin that grace may abound? God forbid. (Rom. 6:1–2)

> For God hath not called us to uncleanness, but unto holiness. (1 Thess. 4:7)

Some pastors would preach that Jesus spent three days in hell to take our punishment. There are no words for those that would add to scripture in such a manner other than what Revelation warns of the consequences of this (Rev. 22:18). Others still will announce that you can pray to someone besides God or Jesus. Praying to saints or Mary is creating an idol. There is only one mediator between God and man, and that is Jesus. Since Revelation and 1 Thessalonians inform the people that the dead in Christ are asleep until the Resurrection and the rapture and the rest of the dead didn't live again until after the millennial reign, then it is obvious Mary and the other saints can't pray for anyone or intercede on anyone's behalf to Jesus (Rev. 20:5; 1 Thess. 4:15).

Unfortunately, there are many that will speak of Jesus being one of many ways to heaven, which is a flat-out lie. As of lately, many have even added that God told them to accept homosexuality now because it is a different day.

The devil uses false prophets daily so that people will follow false doctrine and fall away. Do not be deceived. People shouldn't leave church every single sermon and always feel warm and fluffy inside. At some point, a person should feel convicted. They should feel like the preacher was talking to them, and they need to fix some stuff in their life and get the sin out of it.

A real preacher preaches love and repentance, not love and tolerance. A true prophet will warn of impending doom and to turn from sin before judgment comes. A pastor that is in Christ will tell his sheep about heaven and hell and that Jesus said not everyone that says "Lord, Lord" will make it and only those that walk the narrow path get to hear, "Well done, good, faithful servant" (Matt. 7:21).

Matthew points out that iniquity will abound and the love of many will wax cold. Look at the world today (Matt. 24:12). There is a sense of entitlement everywhere. Everyone feels they are entitled to this instead of having to earn it. The abominations that this world lays before the Lord are too many to count on a daily basis. Women murder the innocent with every abortion. Homosexuality runs rampant and is expected to be celebrated. There are gay pride parades and parties with fake crucifixions of a mock Jesus portrayed by a woman who is kissing another woman. God will not be mocked. That is blasphemy.

Disrespect and crime are more common than hard work and charity. Hatred, drunkenness, and fornication are just part of life for most people. It's as common as the need to change a diaper. The love for Christ and His commandments have left many even though they falsely claim to be Christians. Then there are those that just stopped lying about it because so many think it's cool to be secular instead of a follower of Christ. The numbers of people that identify as Christians have dropped by 8 percent according to Daniel Burke and CNN. More than a third of millennials do not identify with any faith ("Millennials Leaving the Church"). The love of many shall wax cold. The falling away is happening now. There are even churches opening across the lands that worship Satan—some that allow homosexual ministers and some that even represent Christian yoga, which is a Hindu ritual that prepares your body for the acceptance of demon possession.

Many see no need to repent of their sins at all, such as one Republican candidate for president has said in the past. It is a requirement to repent of your sins to be a born-again Christian. Those that haven't aren't really Christians. The Bible sets forth certain things that must be done. The assertion that a saint who points out someone's sin and urges them to repent are then showing hate has become a movement stemming from that false doctrine.

Real love is warning that person before they stand before the Lord at judgment so it can be fixed before it is too late. Everyone is meant to use the scripture for correcting and reproving brothers and sisters in Christ and instructing each other in righteousness (2 Tim. 3:16). Reprove, rebuke, and exhort with all long-suffering is another support verse (2 Tim. 4:2). Titus even says rebuke them sharply that they may be sound in faith (Titus 1:13). It is okay to be angry at sin as long as anger doesn't cause a person to sin. Jesus himself was angered in the temple, pulled out a whip, and started turning over tables, and He was without sin. Anger with blasphemy and sin in this manner are within the realm of possibilities and are acceptable.

> They profess that they know God; but in works
> they deny him, being abominable, and disobedi-
> ent, and unto every good work reprobate (Titus
> 1:16).

Most churches and people that claim to be part of the body of Christ profess that the Bible doesn't apply to today. They are convinced by false doctrine that demons don't exist; the only gospel of Christ is the gospel of love with no repentance needed. They don't believe God will judge anyone or that the gift of speaking in tongues is of God.

They refute the ability to lay hands on the sick and heal or cast out demons through the power of the name of Jesus. Agape love, true love, comes from having a relationship with Jesus himself. Most don't feel you need a relationship with God or Jesus and that going to church or doing a good deed will suffice. This is the love of many waxing cold. They have forgotten their first love, who is Christ.

Last but not least of the signs before the abomination that causes desolation, in Matthew is the message that the gospel will be preached to all nations (Matt. 24:14). Now there have been numbers that insist the world couldn't be in the last days because every person hasn't heard the gospel. Once again, scripture is being changed or taken out of context, which is dangerous and in error. This verse does not say to all people but to all nations.

With the ability of television and the Internet, combined with the missionaries that travel the globe, all nations have now received the gospel of Jesus Christ. In December of 2002, Mary Craig Ministries even went to Antarctica and preached the love of Jesus to anyone that could be found (Craig, "Complete the Mandate"). They even preached to the penguins, fulfilling the order to share Jesus with all of creation. From the North Pole to South Pole and the expanse of the equator, the gospel has been spread to all nations everywhere. The verse says that after this, the end will come.

How does this compare to other scripture throughout the Bible? Just as a single verse should be taken in context with the rest of its chapter, each book and verse should be compared to other books in the Bible. The New Testament must be cross-referenced with the Old Testament, the gospels must be compared to the epistles, and so on.

CHAPTER 3

What Do Other Scriptures Say about the Last Days?

A GOOD PLACE TO START in scripture that were not the words of Christ Himself is in the book of 1 Thessalonians (1 Thess. 5:1–4). Here Paul gives some clues to the coming day of the Lord. This whole chapter contains vital information, but for the sake of specific subjects, for now just concentrate on verses 1–4. The rest will be tackled shortly as it pertains to the subject spoken on.

> But of the times and the seasons, brethren, ye have no need that I write unto you. For yourselves know perfectly that the day of the Lord so cometh as a thief in the night. (1 Thess. 5:1–2)

Paul knows Jesus already focused on the seasons. He writes that there is no need for him to speak on it. Followers of Jesus know all too well it will come like a thief in the night. Not even Jesus knows the hour or the day. God the Father is the only one that knows exactly when it all ends. Jesus is sitting at God's right hand next to the throne of the Almighty, waiting for the word *go*. The next two verses reveal an important piece of information.

> For when they shall say, Peace and safety; then sudden destruction cometh upon them, as travail upon a woman with child; and they shall not escape. But ye, brethren, are not in the darkness,

that the day should overtake you as a thief. (1 Thess. 5:3–4)

Now notice the word *peace* is capitalized. This has significant meaning in itself. This remark "Peace and safety" refers to the prophet Daniel and the peace treaty that will be signed to begin the seven-year tribulation period known as Jacob's trouble (Dan. 9:27). At this time, the whole world will be praising this treaty as groundbreaking and long awaited. This treaty has multiple purposes. It will deceive the masses into thinking all is well. This treaty will be signed by the Antichrist and end-time Israel.

It could have other signatures on it as well but most likely will reveal the Antichrist's identity to Spirit-filled, born-again Christians. This revealing sets in motion a series of many prophecies, all of which come like birth pangs. That reference is supported and repeated here because it is crucial. None of the saints of the Most High will be surprised by the Second Coming of Jesus. No one will know the hour or the day, but they will have already discerned the signs of the times and followed the instructions and guidance of the Holy Spirit that has kept them safe to that point. They will not be in darkness over the matter.

Like many things in scripture, this verse has a double meaning as well. It also conveys that as the body of Christ, there isn't anyone that is walking in darkness. They walk in the light of Jesus, our Savior. So why would it say that? It means even if you didn't discern the times and tribulation and Christ's return did surprise you, there is salvation in Jesus and your heart was already saved so the consequences wouldn't be that of someone not born again. That person's faith probably wasn't prepared, or their house, but if they died unexpectedly in the chaos leading up to the return, there was figuratively nothing for the thief to steal. That person's soul already belonged to Jesus and couldn't be left to the enemy.

Now how does that relate to what is going on today? One requirement of the treaty is that the land of end-time Israel itself must be on one side of this treaty. Israel is currently under constant attack from the Palestinians, Hamas, and being threatened by Muslims all over the world. There are weekly deaths in the streets. There are mortar shells landing in Israeli territory by the handfuls. The United Nations and most of its members are hounding Israel relentlessly. Every time the Palestinians attack, they accuse Israel of human rights violations or some other preposterous notion. The consensus of most nations is that Israel should just cave. They must be in the wrong.

The global community is trying their best to force a two-state agreement. There will eventually be some upper hand by a permanent member state of the Security Council, and they will drop that hand. France is currently trying to bring a resolution before the Security Council that would force a deadline for the treaty. The United States has always remained strong in exercising their veto power to stand with Israel. Until now, this country has had a president that unquestionably stood beside Israel. President Obama has declared that he isn't sure that he can continue to do that anymore. Without an American veto, Palestine has bolstered enough support to push a resolution through if the timing and conditions are right—possibly even force a resolution that defined the terms of the treaty.

Israel could refuse to sign it, but it could be threatened with war, sanctions, withholding of American defense aid, or any number of things that could influence their decision. It isn't a matter of if there will be a two-state agreement but *when* it will happen. Revelation 11 tells us Jerusalem will be divided. The new temple will not include the outer court. It will belong to the Gentiles—the non-Christian Gentiles. This is reinforced by other prophetic scripture as well. Everything is being prepared, set up perfectly like a game of chess waiting for the precise moment to act. These are all reasons that the saints already know it's at the door. It is obvious that the world has been turning against Jerusalem long before the treaty. It is plain as day that the signs in the Bible are all lining up in consecutive order this time. It will not come as a thief in the night to those that stay sober and watch in Christ.

That brings the discussion to Thessalonians and yet another warning about not being deceived (2 Thess. 2:1–3). The more the Bible repeats it, the more detrimental it is. The chapter starts with the words "now we beseech you." Paul is begging brothers and sisters in Christ not to be shaken or troubled. Do not be afraid of the day of the Lord. There is no need for fear in the mind or a person's spirit to be troubled if it is completely surrendered to the Lord Jesus Christ. What is coming will not harm any person that is a born-again Christian and baptized in the Holy Spirit except for persecution as long as they obey.

The reason obedience is key resides in the instructions that will be given by the Holy Ghost, true prophets, and watchman in these last days. These instructions are part of how safety will be obtained. This is why the Bible discloses the outpouring of the Holy Spirit described in Joel and Acts (Joel 2:28–29; Acts 2:17–18). People will dream dreams and see visions for this very reason. Receiving these things is a direct download of instructions, guidance, and expectations from God, so it will not come on His children when they're unprepared.

First and foremost, do not be deceived by false doctrine. The doctrine of men will trick many into not being ready, not keeping a relationship with Jesus, or something worse. Look carefully at Thessalonians (2 Thess. 2:3). The words "that day shall not come" are in italics. The day of the Lord and our gathering unto Him or rapture cannot happen until the falling away occurs and the Antichrist is revealed. It doesn't just say the Second Coming can't happen until these things pass. Paul adds "the gathering together unto Him" to the first verse. This is a specific warning that will be explored in depth toward the end. Regardless for now the sequence of events according to Paul in this passage are the falling away, and then the Antichrist is revealed. It goes on to describe more about the Antichrist, which will be broken down as the story gets there. For now, there is more information that needs to be attended to concerning before tribulation starts.

Paul knew that the most crucial words to listen to are those of the Spirit. When the Holy Ghost speaks, listen. Paul elaborates on specific details that he heard from the Spirit in Timothy (1 Tim. 4:1–5). The Spirit told him that, in the latter times or the last days, some will depart from faith. This constitutes the lack of belief in the ability to cast out demons, laying of hands for healing, speaking in tongues, or gifts of the Spirit that are discussed in 1 Corinthians (1

Cor. 12:7–10). Many lose faith in what God's Word said is possible and in the authority given to each of His children that accept Jesus.

Paul next mentions giving heed to seducing spirits, which are unclean spirits. Examples of these spirits in everyday life can be seen everywhere. These demons whisper lies, deceit, and trickery into people's lives in the forms of subtle things. That's why Genesis calls the devil cunning or subtle (Gen. 3:1). They use things that would appear to be harmless but, in actuality, are literally seducing men, women, and children away from God little by little. The unforgiving spirit causes people to invite other demons into their house, lives, and bodies just by opening a door for them. Matthew tells the church that in order for God to forgive sins, each person must first forgive those that have sinned against them (Matt. 6:15). By not doing so, it is as if they have left the door wide open and anything can walk right in.

How many people today practice yoga? Yoga is a Hindu ritual used to make the body more accepting of spirits that wish to enter that body. It is in itself a demonic worship ritual. Every time someone does yoga, they not only invite unclean spirits to possess them but also participate in the worship of the false god Brahma, whom Hindu believers worship.

Another great tool of demons or seducing spirits is television, movies, and music. The spirit of lust is attached to all sexually explicit or seductive entertainment. Violent, action, and horror movies and shows that contain blood, guts, and gore or even just a lot of fighting is a link to the spirits of rebellion, violence, murder, hate, pride, division, the lying spirit, and many others. There are spirits of doubt, rejection, unbelief, infirmity, anxiety, depression (and the list goes on) attached to these things that people watch religiously and indoctrinate their mind with.

Beyoncé gives a perfect example. She admits when she takes the stage that something takes over, and she has named her Sasha Fierce. It is visually noticeable if someone is paying attention. Her eyes go black, and her face contorts to an evil appearance. This is demon possession being used to sway the masses into seductive dancing and dress. It causes most to dress provocatively, try to seduce or control men, and commit fornication or adultery. Satan was Lucifer before he fell from heaven and grace. He was the angel of light and music and was a perfect beauty. Of course, the devil is going to use his strengths to his advantage.

Many other seducing spirits are apparent with many gateways. Who is addicted to video games, their phone, that gambling hall, making money, work, alcohol, drugs, or any other thing similar to this list? Those have become false idols, and they are being worshiped. Walk away.

What about New Age practices? Transhumanism or raising yourself to a higher plane spiritually—that is demonic. Astrology, horoscopes, tarot cards, spirit guides, psychics, and mediums are all the spirits of divination. Don't open that door either. A Christian has no place doing any of these things, starting with yoga. Anyone else shouldn't engage in them either. They don't even have the covering of the blood of Jesus to protect them.

Occult influences, like the UFO clubs, counterculture cults, human potential movement, holistic divinity, channeling (even with angels), transcendental meditation, spiritual authority of self (I am my own I am), astral projection (you can't take yourself to heaven for a visit), clairvoyance of any kind, ESP, cosmic wisdom, Eastern meditation, and yes, even alternative medicine, mind-altering drugs, and holistic healing are all part of the New Age movement, which use demonic spirits to "access the universe." Do not be involved with any of these things. They leave a person open to demonic attacks and lead to false-doctrine acceptance.

All the things above are doctrines of devils, but doctrines aren't limited to just those things. The devil can take something the Bible says and twist it the slightest bit and make it be so far against God that he doesn't have to do anything else but get someone to fall for that. For example, if the church were to believe the wrong doctrine on when the rapture would occur, then they might not be prepared for the end of days and could be deceived and would fall away. If the body of Christ falls for the "once saved, always saved" doctrine, then they would go on sinning on purpose and living opposite of how Christ commands and could be found lukewarm and vomited out of the body of Christ. If someone were to believe that Jesus was just a teacher and not the Son of God or that He isn't the only way to heaven, then it doesn't matter if they believe every other word in the Bible and follow it to the tee.

So many things could alter the end result dramatically. That's why it is imperative that each person study God's Word in the Bible for themselves with the guidance of the Holy Spirit. Prime examples of these devil's doctrines and lies in hypocrisy lie in Jehovah's Witnesses that believe in salvation by works, Mormons that believe Jesus and the devil are brothers, Seventh-Day Adventists that believe sinners are destroyed and do not go to the lake of fire or hell, Hebrew Roots movement members that have reverted to living under the law, any Catholic that prays to saints or Mary or worships or makes an idol out of anything but Jesus and God the Father, and Calvinism. Now this doesn't mean everyone that claims these denominations but only those that hold to the beliefs listed that are in contradiction of scripture.

It doesn't matter if someone says an angel or God Himself visited and told them to change this doctrine or that. God is the same yesterday, today, and tomorrow. Jesus doesn't change. What the Bible says is truth, and there is no teacher that can change that. Nephilim were the children of women and fallen angels not aliens from the planet Nibiru. Christ doesn't return two more times. There is no need to change the Bible to accept homosexuality. Jesus preached love and repentance, not love and tolerance. Not accepting someone's sin does not equal hatred of the person.

Spreading the gospel isn't shoving anything down someone's throat; it's the ultimate show of love for them. It is also not just the pastor's job but every single Christian's job, and that can be found in Timothy (2 Tim. 4:2, 5). Water baptism doesn't put you under the law. It is a show of faith and that each saint is crucified and rose again as a new creature with Jesus. Don't have a conscience that is seared with a hot iron because that's what the pastor preached. What does God's Word say? When judgment day comes, that pastor can't stand next to anyone and say, "Well, I told them this was true, so it isn't their fault." God's going to say, "Tough they had a Bible available."

The intention is not to upset anyone. Please know that. The only intention is to spread the truth that is in scripture. Further explanation on each thing above is available. There is a warning going out through the land about false doctrine because Jesus doesn't want anyone to be deceived. Love is the only motivation behind truth.

In the last days, people will give heed to spirits that forbid them to marry and command them to abstain from meats. Fornication runs wild in this day. It is more customary to live together than it is to get married. In *Strong's Concordance*, the word used for *forbid* in Greek is *kwluw*, and it is defined as "a means to prevent by word or act, forbid, hinder, keep from, let, not suffer, withstand." The act of fornication prevents people from marrying by the act of sex before marriage. For most, the attitude is "Why buy a ticket when the ride is free?"

Now as for not eating meats, that is part of the Hebrew Roots Movement. There is nothing wrong with going back to the roots of the faith. If a church wants to celebrate the Feast of Tabernacles or Day of Atonement, great—go for it. However, when it goes so far as to put the church back under the law instead of grace and the New Covenant, then there is a problem. It is the law that says one can't eat pork or shrimp or other certain meats. The church is under the New Covenant now, not the law. As long as the meat is received with thanksgiving of those who are born-again Christians and they pray and bless the food to the Lord in Jesus's name, then all creatures are acceptable for eating. This is the whole reason people are supposed to say grace before eating. It isn't just manners, but it keeps the food from being harmful in any way, and that it is given to God not idols. Prayer sanctifies the food. There is power in prayer in all aspects of life. It keeps everyone doing what they need to do.

In general, one can look around at the attitudes and behaviors of the world and deduce that the end is near. The next scriptural evidence supports more of Matthew and collaborating passages as to iniquity abounding and the love waxing cold (Matt. 24).

"This know also in the last days perilous times will come" (2 Tim. 3:1–15). In this passage, Paul lists some behaviors that are signs in themselves as more and more people act like this, and it seems normal (2 Tim. 3:1–5). Men will be lovers of their own selves. Selfies, personal days, spa treatments, vanity, and concentrating on appearances embody this concept. "What do I get out of it?" "What about me—what's in it for me?" No one is supposed to be so stuck on themselves. The Bible says I must decrease and Jesus must increase. There shouldn't be sermons about self-esteem. They should be about self-denial.

No one will keep a promise or a truce, and false accusers abound. How many women cry rape just because they got mad at someone? How many people are framed for someone else's crime? There was a young lady that carried a mattress around a college campus recently, and now she is famous but we come to find out the guy didn't rape her. That's just one example.

People will be fierce and will become despisers of those that are good. Common practice today is a fight over everything. There are riots in the streets, fights in schools, neighborhoods, everywhere. Are these actions condemned or looked down on? No. As fierce as these are, what are seen as inappropriate is the Christian preaching the gospel on the street corner. It's the military man that stopped the rape of a young child in Afghanistan because it went against policy that is punished. It's the county clerk that refuses to sign a marriage license because it goes against the Bible and the baker that refused to bake the cake that are looked at as evil. The brother or sister in Christ that pointed out someone's sin is considered full of hate, while the protester that bashed in a police car is fine. Woe to those that call evil good and good evil.

The traitors, the snooty, and the extremely intelligent people that don't really know anything but stuff that doesn't matter or can't be proven are abundant. The lusts of the flesh or lovers of pleasure are as common as clouds in spring. Go to the club and get drunk, high, hooked up, or whatever. Pop that pill, make that money, work out and get that perfect body—whichever pleasure is the trend of the week is all that matters. It is all that matters because they are lovers of pleasures more than lovers of God. Half or more of them even claim to be Christians, which puts them in the category of the next verse too.

Having a form of godliness but denying the power thereof is right up that alley. They confess the Lord with their mouth but not by their actions. Stay away from these people. That is a direct order in these verses. That's how people fall away. They hang around the wrong crowd. They keep learning all this stuff but are never able to gain any true knowledge, which is the truth in the Word of God. These people will get no further than life in the flesh and the pride of life. Eternity in heaven will pass them by unless they repent and turn to God. If Christians stick to truth in doctrine and fruit of the Spirit, they will know life. It goes on to say that Paul suffered persecutions and so will every single person that is truly living their life for Jesus and doesn't fall under the category of having a form of godliness (2 Tim. 3:11–12). The passage continues showing evil men will get worse and worse. They will continue to deceive and be deceived. The church's orders are to know who they are learning things from and to test the spirits to know the Holy Scripture that makes people truly wise and bring them to salvation through Jesus Christ.

More signs of the times can be seen in Timothy as it mainly supports points that have already been made (2 Tim. 4:2–5). The time will come when no one wants to hear sound doctrine. They just want to sit in the church and have their ears tickled by preachers that tell them exactly what they want to hear. After their own lusts, they look for teachers that do not preach repentance but only love, that preach "once saved, always saved" or that their church has the keys to wealth. God doesn't want His children to be wealthy. He wants us to sell everything above the basics and give it to the poor. That doesn't mean each Christian should live in poverty, just not in luxury.

Paul says they will turn away from the truth and turn to fables, to concocted lies. False prophets will tell them exactly what they want to hear, and they will choose that church over the one that tells them to not drink, to not do drugs, to not go clubbing, to spend more time having a relationship with Jesus than in worldly things, to stop buying diamonds or having manicures and thousand-dollar shoes and clothes, and that they don't need an expensive yacht or fancy car. Also for the following verse, see the parable in Matthew 19:21–24.

> It is easier for a camel to go through the eye of a
> needle than it is for a rich man to enter into the
> kingdom of God. (Mark 10:25)

Most of the church needs to wake up. If the church preaches nothing but things that make the congregation feel warm and fuzzy and never about sin and repentance or heaven and hell, maybe it's the wrong church. A sermon should convict people of their sins and make them want to walk the narrow path Jesus laid out for saints.

In the last days, there will be scoffers walking after their own lusts. There will be many that make fun of the church for preaching the truth or that spew hateful words at the body of Christ for calling out sin or warning that Jesus is coming back soon. There will be those that put the saints down and warn these are the last days and tribulation is coming. There will even be scoffers that claim to be in the church that have been deceived by false doctrine. They will scorn, scowl, and accuse true Christians of blasphemy and being a false prophet because they teach the truth of the Bible. They don't teach what their preacher taught them or the version that makes them feel safe and secure. They will say, "If—as people have been saying for a long time—the end of the world is coming, then where is He already? Everything is the same as when the world started spinning. You are crazy." They will be willingly ignorant that judgment is coming (2 Pet. 3:2–13). It reminds the people that, to God, a thousand years are like a day and that a day is like a thousand years. God is being patient with everyone so that as many as possible might be saved. God wants all to come to repentance. The day of the Lord is coming. The heavens and earth will pass away and melt with fervent heat, and there will be a new heaven and a new earth.

CHAPTER 4

What Prophecy Has Been Fulfilled?

SO MANY OLD AND NEW Testament prophecies have already been fulfilled or are currently in the process of fulfillment. This isn't all of them by any means. They will be divided into fulfilled or in the process of being fulfilled.

First, those prophecies that have already been fulfilled shows where in the prophetic crunch the world is. Every prophecy contains a true story being told before it happens. This will help determine where in the story society is.

The leading scripture attended is Isaiah; it says Damascus is taken away from being a city and is a ruinous heap. The cities of Aroer will be for flocks. The fortress or strength will no longer exist in Ephraim and Syria (Isa. 17:1–3). Now parts of Ephraim would be included in the West Bank, including the city of Ephraim. Syria is still the same area. Both are obviously not the strongholds they were. Syria is definitely no longer a fortress, and the West Bank belongs to Israel even though Palestinians claim it's occupied by them. It came under Israeli control in 1967 during the Six-Day War (History.com staff, "Six-Day War Ends"). This was during what some believe to be the year of Jubilee, which is extremely prophetic itself as addressed by Jonathan Cahn in *The Mystery of the Shemitah* (p. 271). By looking at Damascus itself, it can be seen that the city lies in ruins. It is demolished. Most assuredly, it is a ruinous heap, which fulfilled this prophecy in the last four years of the Syrian Civil War. Most of it was leveled by 2013. That isn't the only part of this prophecy that is active. There is more to be included in the section on prophecies currently being fulfilled.

Next on the list is another passage from Isaiah. It doesn't matter who a person is—how rich, poor, powerful, intelligent, or honorable (Isa. 3:1–16). All of the people of Israel, including the body of Christ, are being oppressed by the secular world. The youth are disrespectful know-it-alls to their elders. The immoral people treat those with biblical principles like a disease to society. The people will point out anyone that made some money to be a leader of the people. A prime example of that is the Trump candidacy. This, having nothing to do with a political stance either way, shows that the people are striving for someone that isn't even in the profession of leading in the political ring. Trump is a billionaire, so the people assume he is capable. He has clothes; let him rule (Isa. 3:6).

They want anyone to blame the judgment that is coming on with the hopes that each new inexperienced choice can solve the problems. The prophecy states that Jerusalem and Judah, symbolizing the unity of physical Israel and spiritual Israel, are fallen because they speak and act in ways that are not of God. The whole world declares their sin proudly. They announce that an abomination is no longer a sin, just like they did in Sodom. They don't even try to hide it anymore. In ancient days, Sodom and Gomorrah were proud of their homosexuality. Gay pride is a direct fulfillment of this (Isa. 3:9).

It warns woe unto their soul, for they reward themselves with evil. Though this society is good to assure equal rights for women, this prophecy declares that when women and children rule over the men, it is in error. As nation after nation elects women as leaders of countries and households, have women running things instead of the man, it displeases God. That doesn't mean women can't have an integral part in government or the family. The ruler of the country or home should be a man. There are cases when there isn't a man in the house. There are always exceptions. How can a widow let the man run the house?

Then Isaiah says judgment is coming to those that are currently extorting the poor for all they have, becoming rich off them instead of helping (Isa. 3:14). Then the last part turns to haughty women that are condescending, stuck up, extravagant, lustful, and immoral, walking around decked out in expensive, seductive clothes and jewelry. They look to attract men to do their bidding by lustful means and bask in the power of the devil. All this describes today perfectly. Most don't even realize some of the prophecy that has already come to pass.

Isaiah contains many things that are already fulfilled even though they continue (Isa. 5:1–23). Houses are built so close to each other in cities across the globe. Each field meets another field with few places left that are wild. So many houses are empty, just lying vacant (Zeph. 1:13–18). So many farms, but they still are not producing enough food, so much so that in the United States, there are subsidies. It profits a farmer more to lose his crop than it does to have a successful one. People wake up and start drinking to get drunk and do so until they pass out at bedtime. They hold feasts and parties to celebrate God but forget to invite Him or even acknowledge it is about Him.

Christmas parties no longer have Christ in them. The resurrection has become Easter, which is a pagan god's name, and has been made about bunnies and dyed eggs. This was a pagan ritual where they sacrificed a rabbit to the pagan goddess of fertility, Ishtar, Oestre, and other names (but all with the pronunciation of Easter). They then took eggs, which were a symbol of the child they wanted to bear, and dipped them in the blood of sacrifice, dying them red ("Hebrew Roots"; McDougall, "Pagan Roots of Easter"; Moftah, "Spring Equinox"). So instead of reading the crucifixion story at a feast and thanking Jesus for salvation, even the churches are now engaging in rituals to false gods and idols in what are supposed to be feasts unto God and Jesus.

Thanksgiving has become about the idol of money and shopping instead of based on the thankfulness of God, providing for a new nation that would be established in a covenant with Him. The Feast of Tabernacles, Day of Atonement, and Feast of Trumpets are rarely celebrated except those of Jewish descent that haven't accepted Christ as the Messiah. Many of God's people have gone into captivity of sin. They have no knowledge of the things that are important.

They only know worldly things. Iniquity and sin have multiplied so much that hell has enlarged itself to accommodate those that are falling away.

In 2013 the uprising in Egypt and the leaders that were in power at that moment and leaders that took power during, accomplish one prophecy. The Egyptians were at each other's throats. Their rulers had such bad intentions there were riots and criminal charges brought against one in court. This is clearly the verses from Isaiah. (Isa. 19:1–4). Egypt continually seeks the false god Allah for help and answers to the division and death.

The completion of one prophecy started around AD 630–650 and was finished in 1948 (Hosea 3:4–5). Many Islamic caliphates controlled Israel except for the Crusade period, ending with the Ottoman Empire in the early 1900s. It was reestablished as the country of Israel in 1948, and the Jewish people started returning in floods. They even began to speak Hebrew, a language that had been unused by most for over a thousand years. This completely revived the origins of God's chosen people except for a third temple, which isn't mentioned in this prophecy.

The people are destroyed for lack of knowledge as the world has forgotten God's laws (Hosea 4:6–17). As the population increases around the world, so does sin. The people will eat and not have enough. Obesity runs rampant as well as eating disorders. They will commit whoredom and not increase. Fornication and pregnancy out of wedlock is a common thing, and sinners have a common solution. It has become so common that a political party in the United States stands in defense of it and the taxpayers are forced to fund it. Between birth control and abortion, many are free to commit fornication without consequences as they see it without increasing their family size. The consequences are actually greater than realized.

They have accepted the spirit of whoredom in their midst and are controlled by this demon to a point of even cheating on God. There are idol sacrifices and worshipping across the lands to many idols and false gods even by some that insist they are Christian. Newsflash: one can't be a Christian and a witch, and there is no such thing as white magic. Fornication and adultery are widespread. The church and physical Israel are backsliding. No one reads their Bible anymore to have the true knowledge of God, but instead they listen to a preacher tickling their ears with false doctrine. They are being led astray and don't even realize it because they don't study the Word for themselves.

Lack of knowledge has destroyed many. Hosea elaborates on this prophecy and adds that the "revolters" slaughter people even though they have been rebuked (Hosea 5). It also adds that the Jewish people have mixed their blood with others and begotten strange children. The Lord wanted the twelve tribes of Israel kept pure. Certain tribes had certain jobs. As they prepare for the third temple, there has been trouble proving lineage and pure blood of the tribe of Levi to show the right and ability to be a priest in the temple.

The book of Joel holds important prophetic events. It says that the priests and ministers will call the congregation together and plead for everyone to drop what they're doing and fast and pray (Joel 2:15–17). The leaders of the churches that stand true to God are begging this nation and the world to repent and turn to God. They are crying out to God to not let heathens influence and rule over His people. Joel declares that Palestine has stolen from the Israeli people and sold them off as slaves (Joel 3:4–10). God states that if they will not make recompense, then He will heap it back on their head and they will belong to Israel. The Palestinian territories are now under Israeli control, and their government funds were withheld for a few years until Benjamin Netanyahu agreed to release part of it in 2015. It says proclaim among the Gentiles to prepare for war (Joel 3:9). Turn plowshares into swords. This is the call among the Palestinians as they encourage stabbing attacks in Israel and considering the intifada (Protective Edge in 2014); this prophecy is complete.

Israel will never be removed from its land again according to Amos (Amos 9:15). Also Amos decrees that out of the multitude that left Israel, only a remnant has survived and are returning, which is about 10 percent (Amos 5:3–10). Those that seek the Lord have found everlasting life, and those that seek the idols are in the captivity of sin. Those that stand in the cities and rebuke sin are hated, and those that speak truth are utterly abhorred. This has most certainly come to pass and really could be included in part in the ongoing events as well. This remnant is also spoken of in Micah (Mic. 5:1–8). This also says that God gives the people up to be scattered until the time which she travaileth hath brought forth. In other words, the remnant of Israel returning, the Aaliyah, won't happen until the birth pangs spoken of in Matthew are in effect (Matt. 24). This is reinforcement that the rebirth of Israel starts the end times and the last generation. This is another reason when reading the Bible, things must always be taken in context—not only of the surrounding verses, but the Bible as a whole. This is the New Testament being explained by Old Testament prophecy and vice versa.

From this point on, Israel will be a great nation despite its size among the world. The Assyrian (Mic. 5:5) represents the terrorists just like the harbingers in Isaiah (Isa. 9:9–11) also spoken of by Jonathan Cahn (p. 34–42). The first terrorist to Israel came from the Assyrian Empire. Their actual land is modern-day Syria and part of Iraq, but spiritual Assyria is anyone that wants Israel to cease to exist.

Micah refers to the land of Syria and the western portion of Iraq (Mic. 5:6). This is also equivalent to the territories of ISIS, which is another instance of a double meaning of scripture in the Bible. Western Iraq and all of Syria is a wasteland from war right now, but the land of Israel sits in the midst of it all, standing strong as a lion. Those that come against Israel have been halted by the mighty hand of God. There has even been a news article where the factions in the Gaza Strip have said they fire rockets at Israel but their God bats them down. Within the dual meaning, all the nations surrounding Israel, Egypt, Syria, Jordan, Iraq, and Lebanon, supported by other Muslim nations, Algeria, Kuwait, Libya, Morocco, Pakistan, PLO, Sudan, and Tunisia, attacked Israel together. This war was over in six days, and Israel regained Jerusalem, the Sinai Peninsula, the Gaza Strip, the West Bank, and the Golan Heights by the will and awesome hand of God (History.com staff, "Six-Day War Ends"). Once again, the remnant of Jacob prevailed in the midst of many people like a lion without waiting on help from any man.

There are quite a few in Zephaniah. One has been partially fulfilled in reference to Gaza (Zeph. 2:4). Gaza is just as desolate as

Damascus. Ashkelon is part of the Jewish-occupied territories and receives rocket fire from Gaza on a regular basis but is standing. Another one in Zephaniah is complete in the fact that there is nothing left of Syria after this war, and Nineveh no longer exists (Zeph. 2:13–14). Its ruins are across the river from Mosul, Iraq, which is in and out of ISIS control as of late. Even the ruins are taking fire. A prophecy mentioned in Zephaniah and Matthew was fulfilled in AD 70, when the Roman Empire destroyed the temple and stole all the treasures from it (Zeph. 1:7–13; Matt. 24:12). That also overtook the princes and rulers of Israel, and eventually the palaces were empty when they fled Jerusalem after a revolt from the Jewish people that started in AD 66, in which most of Jerusalem was burned to the ground.

Probably one of the most important things to discuss is in Ezekiel (Ezek. 36, 37). The first chapter addressed concerns the actual land of Israel (Ezek. 36). God says that He will make the desert and mountains bloom for the children of Israel. The cities will fill up, and Israel will increase. The children of the land of Israel will have better crops and more livestock and hunting than before. Before God was angry and scattered the people in judgment, but now He will gather them out of all countries and bring them to their own land. He will cleanse the people and give them a new heart and a new spirit. He will turn their heart of stone into a heart of flesh and put His Spirit in them, which will cause them to walk in His statutes. He says they will dwell in the land He gave them and be His people and He will save them from uncleanness. The land will be tilled and fruitful, and the heathen will be all around them.

As the Jewish people were scattered, they were never really known as farmers. The land of Israel has been next to impossible to farm all these years, but in 1948, something changed. God's people started coming home, and the people that couldn't farm made the land that couldn't be farmed bloom and bring forth much harvest. Right now many Jewish people are being saved, cleansed, and given a new heart and the Holy Spirit as they finally accept Jesus Christ as the Messiah. After all these centuries, their hearts are no longer hardened to the Messiah, who came to save them. They are accepting Jesus at an enormous rate and are also putting Romans into play with the original branches being grafted back in to the olive tree (Rom. 11). This leads to the next chapter, which describes the people of Israel as dry bones in the desert (Ezek. 37). With the breath of God, these bones or the people of Israel, a nation that hasn't existed in almost two thousand years, are alive again. The nation of Israel, God's chosen people, is reborn out of the dust.

With this rebirth comes unity. There will no more be the nation of Judah and Israel but one country united as all of Israel, and it will never be divided again. It again repeats the saving of Israel by being cleansed or accepting Jesus. This is known by the reference that David will be king over them. The end of the chapter shows that the temple will be rebuilt a third time in the land of Israel. It's clear it is the third temple because it doesn't appear until after the rebirth of Israel and unification of Judah and Israel as one along with the rise of acceptance in Jesus as the Messiah. It's all about the chronological order of events in determining the last days.

Last but not least, or especially not all, there is the book of Daniel (Dan. 12:4, 8–11a). Knowledge in the worldly sense has increased exponentially since the Information Age began with the Digital Revolution starting in the 1950s (Dan. 12:4). Notice the dates there. Israel was reborn in 1948, and knowledge began to increase in the fifties. This is also when the hustle and bustle of life started getting so busy. Everyone was, and still is, running to and fro, trying to get to work, ball games, the gym, and so on. Then there is the time of the end, which is sealed up, and before then, many will be purified and made white (Dan. 12:8–11a). Daniel might not have grasped this, but now it is known that it's by the blood of Jesus that the saints' robes are made white. There are wicked people that continue to do wicked, and they do not understand the gospel of Jesus. Then the daily sacrifice is taken away (Dan. 12:11a). This has all been fulfilled. Now the sacrifices will be taken away again after the third temple is rebuilt, but that will be discussed in prophecy that is yet to be fulfilled.

CHAPTER 5

What Prophecy Is in the Process of Fulfillment?

ANYONE CAN LOOK AROUND AND see that many prophecies are presently underway as long as they know what to look for. For example, the mass animal deaths are occurring globally (Hosea 4:3; Zeph. 1:3). Hosea and Zephaniah state that the birds, beasts, and fish will all be taken away. The evidence of this can be seen everywhere. The large fish, dolphin, and whale die-offs are washing up everywhere. There are mass numbers of other animals dying, such as turtles, antelope, bats, birds, and much more in the news. This will go on until the day of the Lord.

The Bible promises of Aaliyah, or the return of Jewish people to Israel, are noted in Isaiah, Micah, and specifically, that from Ethiopia in Zephaniah (Isa. 11:11–16; Mic. 4:6–7; Zeph. 3:10–11; Zech. 10:6–12). These prophecies are all still ongoing now. The process of them being fulfilled is started and will continue until all have returned. The Jewish people are coming from Ethiopia, Russia, Iraq, Syria, France, Belgium, other parts of Europe, United Kingdom, and from around the globe. So far, the only country that hasn't sent a mass Aaliyah home to Israel is the United States, and it will come.

A very important prophecy is found in Acts and Joel (Acts 2:17–19; Joel 2:28–30). This one began being fulfilled the day of Pentecost, when the first 120 received the Holy Ghost and continues today—though today it is in full force. The Holy Spirit is a gift given to every born-again Christian at the asking. Some receive it the moment they are saved, but as it can be blocked or refused, some do not receive it until they ask for it later, prepared to actually receive it. Preparation simply means one no longer doubts or fears the power of God and wants to receive it. More discussion will go on later. The verses in Acts and Joel tell us that in the last days, men and women, sons and daughters will prophesy, see visions and dreams, and be used for God's work. These are the verses that now allow women to teach, preach, and minister the gospel to all. Acts and Joel point to more signs of the end times in the form of signs in the heavens and in the earth. It also shows there will be volcanoes, which is the reference to blood, fire, and pillars of smoke (Acts 2:17–19; Joel 2:28–30).

At any given time, the Ring of Fire has four to five volcanoes erupting at the same time. Presently, there are forty volcanoes erupting together across the Ring of Fire, and the seismic activity has increased dramatically. Note that there is a point in childbirth when the baby's head is crowning that is also referred to as the ring of fire. This is mentioned due to the metaphor Jesus used when referring to birth pangs or sorrows. The signs in the earth—or earthquakes, sinkholes, and landslides—have been escalating everywhere. They are growing like birth pangs, mounting in intensity and frequency.

There are also currently volcanoes that have been inactive or quiet, swelling and growing their magma expanse in preparation for an eruption. Mount St. Helens is now showing seismic activity, though no expanse in magma, in the form of 130 minor quakes under the volcano. The long dormant and inactive supervolcano at Yellowstone Park has a magma chamber underneath the caldera that has more than doubled in size recently, and the rivers close by have been seen boiling.

The geysers are behaving strangely, and gases have been released in certain areas close by. These are all signs of possible eruption in the future, maybe even near future. Parts of the Yellowstone Park have even been closed to the public for unknown reasons. There has also been a change in the website. Seismic information isn't available immediately as it was previously. There is a twenty-four-hour to forty-eight-hour delay on the release of the data on the official website, and people that live near are claiming it isn't complete or accurate.

They believe data is being withheld. Their claim is that they know they felt a quake at a certain time, but there was no mention of one at all or the tremors that followed.

It also seems relative to note the growth in close calls with asteroids, amount of eclipses, meteorites hitting the earth, the star of Bethlehem reappearing after two thousand years (not once but twice and expected again), and many others signs. There are definitely signs in the earth and sky and an increase in volcanic activity worldwide.

Referring back to Isaiah is notable here. Isaiah can appear cryptic, but the verses in question are very plain. The multitude of many people refers to the large amount of refugees flooding into countries right now. They make noise like the noise of the sea as they are crashing into borders, like waves rushing into nations, like the rushing of mighty waters that can't be stopped. They flee to escape and God rebukes them and they then flee far off, even as far as Canada, Mexico, America, etc. They are chased as the chaff before the wind because they are being judged by God for their iniquity of worshiping a false god. They are labeled as trouble. God also warns these nations here that their purpose is to spoil and rob everyone (Isa. 17:12–14). They are not peaceful, and the people aren't supposed to give them shelter. The refugees are not meant to be let in.

They are supposed to be kept out of our countries with all perseverance. They will tear these countries that take them in apart and bring them to ruin or spoil them. God knew there would be those that said the Christian thing to do would be to help them, but obviously, that is not His will for the situation when He commanded the people otherwise so long ago. God must be talking about the refugees from now and not the past because when the chronological order of things is taken into account in this chapter, it is seen that first Damascus must come to a ruinous heap then they will flood the nations. Are they not labeled Syrian refugees? Are they not fleeing the war that brought Damascus down? How then can a nation let them in without disobeying a command from God not to? By the way, every word in the Bible is a command, not a suggestion.

The book of Zechariah holds many prophetic words for the last days. Jerusalem will be a cup of trembling to all people around her.

They will be in siege with Judah and Jerusalem. God says through Zechariah that the holy city will become a burdensome stone for all people and all that burden themselves with it shall be cut into pieces even though everyone on earth is gathered against them (Zech. 12:1–3).

This portion has great significance for Jerusalem. Right now in the world, many nations are in agreement against Israel. Jerusalem is no longer considered the capital city. There are organizations that promote a multitude of boycotts against products made in Israeli settlements. Even though the Israeli people gained Jerusalem and other territories fairly in the Six-Day War, defending their land and right to exist, most do not think they should keep the land or occupy the areas (History.com staff, "Six-Day War Ends").

The land was given back to the Jewish people by God. The neighboring countries took it upon themselves to attack Israel with the sole purpose of wiping her out. They did not and do not believe Israel has a right to exist at all. Their attack led to a retreat that left these areas under Israeli control fair and square. The whole world wants Israel to return to pre-1967 borders so as not to offend anyone. They believe in the two-state agreement and will force it if necessary.

There are currently resolutions about to be brought before the UN Security Council by France and Palestine that pertain to this and the settlement of Israelis in the West Bank again. There have been many resolutions trying to force a two-state agreement. The United States has always stood with Israel and vetoed these votes, but now the situation may have changed. The world is seeing a global response against Israel for the inhumanity and lies of the Palestinian people even to the point of Israel being accused of war crimes for responding to rockets being fired at them.

Palestine has even managed to be recognized as a state among the UN General Assembly even though they have no land. It is as if the UN recognized Boko Haram as a state because they threw a fit for forty years like a two-year-old. It is simply ridiculous. Some countries have even suggested sanctions against Israel. Iran fired ballistic missiles with the phrase "Israel should be wiped off the Earth" painted on them (Onyanga-Omara, "Reports: Iran Fires Missile").

The nuclear agreement with Iran is a direct threat to Israel, and no one cared. All nations are gathering against Israel. It will culminate in a war that will result in the prophecy of the first Gog and Magog war. This war ends with utter destruction of all the armies that come against Israel. This is not the battle of Armageddon as Israeli soldiers fight in this war; the battle of Armageddon only has soldiers gathered in the valley of Megiddo from the Antichrist's side.

Many get these two wars confused. This moves the topic on to Zechariah in which a third of the people give their hearts to Jesus and are refined in the fire and are true to the Lord (Zech. 13:9). This is the move of the Holy Spirit seen so strongly across the globe right now. All those that claim to be Christians are either turning cold or hot gradually. They are either falling away or being set on fire for Jesus. The area in between hot and cold or the lukewarm Christians are disappearing, and when the Antichrist appears on the scene, those that are left will be separated. Those with names written in the Lamb's book of life will be saved and will know truth. For those that aren't, God will cause them to believe the lies and worship the Antichrist.

This is covered in the 2 Thessalonians (2 Thess. 2:7–12). Those that are not already saved at the start of tribulation will be forced to believe the Devil's lies by God. There is Matthew, Mark, Luke, 2 Thessalonians, 1 Timothy, and 2 Timothy. Don't forget 2 Timothy and 2 Peter (Matt. 24:4–14; Mark 13:5–13; Luke 21:8–19; 2 Thess. 2:1–3; 1 Tim. 3:1–14; 2 Tim. 4:1–6; 2 Peter 2:1–9). There are so many scriptures prophesying things for the end times that are being played out before the eyes of the world. People don't even realize it. They are coming in chronological order with all the right require-ments this time. They can't be refuted by any other scripture. The only arguments are inventions of scoffers that want to remain igno-rant concerning what the Lord says. Are you paying attention, people?

CHAPTER 6

What Is Yet to Be Fulfilled?

IT IS SAFE TO SAY the discussion on these prophecies will be much
more limited as there are so many. Not all of them will even be mentioned, but here goes. Starting with Psalms, this war is thought by
many to have already been fulfilled in the Six-Day War, but that war
was missing a key player (Psalm 83). The players in this war are listed
as Edom, the Ishmaelites, Moab, the Hagarenes, Gebal, Ammon,
Amalek, and the Philistines. In modern day, this breaks down as
Jordan, Saudi Arabia, Egypt, Lebanon, Syria, the Sinai Peninsula,
and Palestine or the PLO. Saudi Arabia was missing from the Six-
Day War. That means this prophecy wasn't fulfilled; however, it is on
the verge of doing so now.

If ISIS, Hezbollah, and Hamas all attack Israel, it will fulfill the
requirements of this war. In an ongoing war on terror, so far Hamas
and Hezbollah have already attacked. This leaves ISIS to claim attacks
there, and ISIS has already recently declared they're coming.

How would these terrorists fulfill this prophecy? Each of these
groups represents each one of these governments in their true feelings
and has their support. They can't express it on the world stage, or they
will be charged with war crimes as well as bring a response on a global
scale of war. No Islamic state believes Israel has the right to exist, and
their prophecy says in the end times Muslims will wipe Israel off the
face of the Earth. God will not be put in a box though. It doesn't
have to come about by these terrorist organizations. It could happen
in any way God sees fit.

Most prophecies can be categorized in some way, and then there are those that seem to fit into more than one or not in one at all. For example, Isaiah speaks of the judgment coming to Babylon and the tents of Kedar. It orders the people to post a watchman (Isa. 21). One thing that needs to be realized is that a prophecy tends to have cycles. The prophecy of Isaiah (Isa. 9:9–11) was fulfilled in Israel back in the time of the Assyrian invasion, but it is repeating itself right now in America (Cahn, *Harbinger*). Some prophecies are given for nations that enter into covenant with the Lord. It can happen more than once. Isaiah portrays the downfall of Babylon and the tents of Kedar in ancient times (Isa. 21). By looking at the previous fulfillment, it gives an idea as to a repeat fulfillment.

In modern day, Babylon would be America, and the tents of Kedar, Media, and Elam would be Saudi Arabia. The prophecy says that within a year, all the glory of Kedar shall fall. Notice also that Isaiah mentions he was overtaken with birth pangs, giving the people a clue this will happen in the last days again (Isa. 21:3). It otherwise would not pain him for a country that held his people in captivity to fall.

He mentions two sets of two horsemen that the watchman warns about. This could also be a reference to the coming four horseman of the apocalypse. These horsemen bring the fall of Babylon with them. It does not give a clue as to when the year that is the deadline for the destruction will start. Now to point out a few other facts, the first time Babylon was defeated was at the hands of the Persians and the Medes.

In modern day, that is Iran and the eastern portion of Iraq. At this moment, as it is 2016, Saudi Arabia and Iran are locked up in a proxy war in Yemen. The glory of Saudi Arabia is Mecca, Islam's most treasured site. Less than a year ago, there was a construction accident where a crane fell on a multitude of people that caused over a thousand deaths and injuries during their "holy" pilgrimage. Iran is also very upset with the Saudi government concerning this issue and will not be allowing Iranian citizens to make the pilgrimage this year. Islamic prophecy states their twelfth imam will crawl out of a well in the desert and march through Israel, taking control of and destroying

Israel on the way to Mecca. Christians know this to be most likely the Antichrist or possibly another crazy false prophet.

The clues that can be taken from this would be that this is a dual prophecy and during the end times, America and Saudi Arabia will be judged and destroyed for their abominations before the Lord. Even Revelation speaks to the judgment of the whore Babylon.

Isaiah foretells a prophecy for Palestine that is known not to be fulfilled simply because they still exist. It declares that a famine will be brought to Palestinians that will dry up the root of Palestine and those that survive it will be slayed (Isa. 14:29–31).

Amos foretells Israel never leaving their land again and that in the same age, the temple will be rebuilt (Amos 9:11–15). This is pointed out to be the last days, where it says that "the plowman overtakes the reaper and the treader of grapes him that soweth seeds" (Amos 9:13). In other words, this is the time when soon the winepress of God's wrath will no longer need Christians to sow seeds but instead Jesus will take over and tread the winepress. There will be no more harvest to reap once rapture has occurred and Jesus has already reaped the harvest.

Next it's going to get a bit complicated in the book of Daniel. There is highly important information here, but it is understood by much study and prayer. Just like Revelation, parts of the book of Daniel can be somewhat cryptic though it does offer a bit more explanation than Revelation does. Daniel receives a vision from the Lord about the last days (Dan. 7:3–27). It is the rise of the beast system here on earth. It would be supported by Revelation as well (Rev. 13). The actual vision in this excerpt is followed by the interpretation by the angel.

Here is a brief overlay of the vision itself. Four beasts come out of the sea. The first one was like a lion and had eagle's wings, and Daniel watched as the wings were plucked and the lion stood up like a man and a man's heart was given to it. The second beast was like a bear raised up on one side, and it had three ribs in its mouth in between its teeth and was told to arise and devour much flesh. The third beast was like a leopard with four wings of a bird on its back and four heads, and dominion was given to it. Then the fourth beast was terrible and exceedingly strong with iron teeth; it devoured and broke into pieces and stamped the residue with its feet, and it had ten horns.

Daniel thought about the horns, and a little horn came up and took the place of three of the horns that were plucked up by their roots. The little horn had the eyes of a man and a mouth speaking great things. Daniel looked until the thrones were cast down, and the Ancient of Days did sit. His garment was white as snow and His hair like wool. His throne was like a fiery flame and His wheels as burning fire. A fiery stream came forth from before Him.

Multitudes stood before Him and a million ministered to Him. The judgment was set, and the books were opened. Daniel looked because the voice of the great words that the horn spoke even till the beast was slain and his body destroyed and given to the burning flame. The rest of the beasts had their dominion taken away, but their lives were prolonged for a season and a time. Then the Son of man came in the clouds and came to the Ancient of Days, and they brought him near before him. He was given dominion, glory, and a kingdom, and all people, nations, and languages should serve him. His dominion is an everlasting dominion that shall not pass away or be destroyed (Dan. 7:3–14).

So this is the vision with all descriptions and almost word for word. Then the interpretation is received. The beasts are four kings or kingdoms that will rise. Ultimately, the saints will take the kingdom forever. The fourth beast has teeth of iron and nails of brass and ten horns and a little horn that came up, before which three fell. The little horn is strong and made war with the saints and prevailed against them until the time came for the saints to possess the kingdom when God makes judgment for the saints.

The fourth beast is a fourth kingdom that will be different from all other kingdoms and devour the whole earth. It will tread it down and break it to pieces. The ten horns are ten kings that will rise, and another king will rise after them; he is different from the first ten and will subdue three of the ten kings.

He will speak great words against the Most High and will wear out the saints. He will think to change times and laws, and they will be given into his hand for a time—times and a dividing of a time. Then judgment shall sit and his dominion taken away. The kingdom and dominion shall be given to the saints (Dan. 7:17–27).

As this is broken down further, there are four kings or world powers. Each of the first three beasts represents a nation or kingdom itself that rise in consecutive order as world powers. They are not necessarily powers that are in control but are recognized as having power in their own right. The Bible doesn't give us the kingdoms but does give us clues. So as each beast is looked at, think about what nation they symbolically associate with.

The first beast is a lion with the wings of an eagle that were plucked off and set on his feet like a man. The lion most likely represents the rise of England. The wings of an eagle would steer most toward America, especially due to the fact they were plucked off the lion. America declares independence from England. These two countries are the first modern faces of civilized, compassionate countries that came to the aid of those in need on a global scale. To this day, they are the first two to help in wars, disasters, and other issues. The compassion and civilized humility represents the heart of a man given to a beast.

The second beast you see is that of a bear. This is agreed across the board among Bible scholars to be Russia. The description of this beast is one of violence, which plays out well to a theory of Russia. The monarchy was lost by force, communism took hold and became a dictator to the people, and they treat the world like they are a bully that can push anyone around to get what they want.

Then the third beast is a four-headed leopard with four wings of a bird. One of the next countries to rise in power was Germany. Though the country recognizes the eagle as its animal, it can still be thought of when there is a leopard. The eagle actually lends to the theory in that it gives us the wings. It was due to Germany that World War I started. They used Leopard tanks in their invasions, so the source of their destruction during this time was the leopard, literally. It just wasn't the animal. This war ended the German Empire along with other empires. There were four central powers in this war: the Ottoman Empire (which ended here), Austria-Hungarian Empire (also ended here), Bulgaria, and of course, the German Empire. That could very well be the four heads of that beast that rose Germany to a serious threat permanently.

The fourth and last empire to rise will be very different. It will be the Antichrist's beast system. It will start by taking over the world by force. Ten kings will rise to power in this system. Then another will come along and subdue three of those original ten kings or kingdoms. This king will be the Antichrist and will blaspheme God. He will change times and laws and persecute and behead the saints for three and a half years until the return of Jesus. At the moment the eleventh king speaks the great words of blasphemy, the great tribulation begins. This is the last three and a half years of the tribulation period. This is all Daniel has shown at this point.

The next prophecy in Daniel is another vision given to him by the Lord. Daniel envisioned he was at the palace Shushan in the province of Elam. It should be noted this palace was 150 miles east of the Tigris River in modern-day Iran. Daniel was under Persian control during the time of these visions. Daniel sees in the vision a ram with two horns; they were high, one higher than the other, and the higher came up last.

The ram pushed westward, northward, and southward. No beast could stand before it. There was no one to deliver a beast from the ram, and it did whatever it pleased and became great. Then a male goat came from the west on the whole face of the earth and never touched the ground. It had a notable horn between its eyes, and he came to the ram that had two horns, which Daniel had seen standing by the river; he ran into him with the full fury of his power.

The goat was moved with rage against the ram and smote the ram and broke his two horns. There was no power in the ram to stand before him, and the goat threw him on the ground and stomped him. Nothing could save the ram from the goat. The goat became very great. When he was strong, the great horn broke, and four notable ones came up toward the four winds of heaven.

Out of them came a little horn that became exceedingly great toward the south, east, and toward the pleasant land. It waxed great even to the host of heaven and cast down some of the host and the stars to the ground and stomped on them. He magnified himself to the prince of hosts and took the daily sacrifice away. The place of his sanctuary was cast down. A host was given to him against the daily sacrifice by reason of transgression, and it cast truth to the ground and practiced and prospered.

One saint said to another, "How long shall be the vision concerning the daily sacrifice and the transgression of desolation to give both the sanctuary and the host to be trodden under foot?" He said, "Two thousand three hundred days and the sanctuary will be cleansed" (Dan. 8:3–14). This is the vision, and once again, an angel shows up to interpret the vision for Daniel (Dan. 8:19–25).

The angel calls it the last indignation and says at the time appointed the end shall be. The ram with two horns are the kings of Media and Persia and the goat is the king or kingdom of Grecia or the Roman Empire and the great horn is the first king. That horn was broken, and four kingdoms shall stand up out of that nation but not in his power.

In the latter time of the kingdom, when the transgressors have come to the full, a king of fierce countenance and understanding dark sentences shall stand up. His power will be mighty but not by his own power, and he will destroy wonderfully and prosper and practice and destroy the holy people. Through his policy, he will cause craft to prosper and magnify himself in his heart and by peace will destroy many. He will stand up against the Prince of princes but will be "broken without hand" (Dan. 8:19–25).

Now this clarifies the first vision somewhat. The simpler version goes like this. The Persian Empire destroyed Babylon and took over everything. Then along came the Roman/Greco Empire and showed the Persians no mercy. With Alexander the Great's death, the Roman Empire was divided and given to his four generals. They did not get the full power of the Roman Empire but simply inherited rather than conquered their thrones. As time went by, it became unclear what exactly the Roman Empire is today.

The latter times or last days arrive when the sinners have reached their fullest. Now comes the unfulfilled part. Out of the Roman Empire, the Antichrist will rise. Now remember the Roman Empire stretched from Morocco to Egypt and up past Turkey and France and then from parts of Iran to Spain, including England. It was vast; therefore, the Antichrist could come from the Roman Empire and still come from an Islamic country easily. Also America is a child of England, so it can also be included in the Roman Empire.

In this vision also, the Antichrist is evil and makes war with the saints, but it also reveals that he doesn't work by his own power. Revelation clarifies that his power comes from the beast or the devil. He will use the guise of peace to conquer and control. Jesus defeats him without raising a hand, and no humans are involved.

This does give some direction as to where the Antichrist will rise from. It rules out many large nations (such as China, Russia, India, Australia, and other eastern or northern territories) as well as the smaller ones that already act like they might be the Antichrist (like North Korea, Pakistan, Afghanistan, and so on).

Daniel gives the Bible one of the most famous end-time prophecies. This states the end of the theory of seventy weeks, which defines tribulation as a seven-year period that begins with a peace treaty or covenant with many. In the middle of this seven-year period, at the three-and-a-half-year mark, the abomination that causes desolation occurs, beginning the great tribulation and persecution of the saints. This is also when daily sacrifices cease, so that defines that the third temple is already rebuilt (Dan. 9:26–27). Revelation adds to that by saying the Antichrist stands in the temple, blaspheming God at the beginning of the great tribulation. There is also very important information in Daniel 11:29–45, but breaking that down would take up entirely too much time in combination with what is still left to address.

There are still other unfulfilled prophecies, such as 2 Thessalonians 2:4–14, Haggai 2:21–23, Isaiah 4, and Micah 4:1–3, all speak to the kingdom after Jesus's return. Isaiah 2, Isaiah 3:17–26, Isaiah 13, Isaiah 24:18–23, Isaiah 27:12–13, James 5:1–7, 2 Peter 3:10–13, Joel 2:1–3 and 9–12 and 31–32, Zechariah 14, Matthew 24:29–31, Mark 13:24–27, and Luke 21:27–28 all cover what the terrible day of the Lord and Armageddon will consist of and be like. The rapture is covered in 1 Thessalonians 5:13–17, Daniel 12:1–2,

Matthew 24:29–31 and 40–51, Mark 13:24–27 and 36–37, and Luke 21:27–28 and 36. Those will be discussed toward the end in more detail.

There are plenty of prophecies foretelling what to expect during the great tribulation as well. Some of those can be found in Zechariah 12:9–14, Matthew 24:15–28, Mark 13:14–23, Luke 21:20–26, and of course, the book of Revelation, which is a whole other book in itself.

Speaking of another book in itself, the first war of Gog and Magog could take up a novel. That just simply isn't possible here. There is an abundance of scripture available on the subject. Some good scripture can be found in Ezekiel 38 and 39, Jeremiah 46:2–10, Ezekiel 30:2–19, Joel 2:19–20, and Joel 3:1–2, 11–15. These passages, when rightly divided and read by the Holy Spirit, will give many key factors that will just be touched on lightly.

First the key players are listed. There is disagreement among scholars as to whether Gog and the chief prince of Meshech and Tubal are one or two rulers. Some argue that Gog is Russia and the chief prince is Turkey, and some say they are one and the same and it is the ruler of Turkey. It all stems from the debate over how the comma is used. For the answer, go to *Strong's Concordance* and the original language the Bible was written in. Gog is the chief prince of Meshech and Tubal.

These are the descendants of Japheth and their land. The proper areas according to scholars to lean to would be East Asia Minor, Armenia in the Syrian times, and in the Persian times near the Black or Euxine Sea. The countries that border that are Bulgaria, Georgia, Romania, Russia, Turkey, and Ukraine. Genesis states that the sons and family of Japheth (including Gomer, Magog, Madai, Javan, Meshech, Tubal, and Tiras) all settled in the isle of the Gentiles (Gen. 10:2–5).

The isles of the Gentiles would be considered the islands and mainland west of Canaan, such as Europe and even as far as England. The isles of the Gentiles in Moses's mind would have been anything past the Mediterranean Sea on the coast of Canaan. It would land those princes south and west of the Black Sea. This would most likely place Gog in the Turkey, Bulgaria, Armenia, Georgia, or Greece areas. Then there is Persia, which consists of modern-day Iran and the Eastern part of Iraq. They are joined by Ethiopia, which today would consist of part of Sudan, South Sudan, Ethiopia, Eritrea, Djibouti, and Somalia. Libya is included and would contain part of modern-day Libya, Algeria, and Tunisia.

Gomer and all his bands and the house of Togarmah of the north quarter are also descendants of Japheth. They would have also spread in the same directions as Meshech and Tubal. Any of the above places could be considered the north quarters. Keep in mind they were separated by languages as well. The founding of Babel was in the same era of time. Language similarities can be a good clue in this situation. Last but not least, Israel will be on the receiving end of this war.

Next, an important piece of data here is that this will take place in the latter years. It also specifies the land of unwalled villages before it outright states Israel. This points to modern-day Israel because the only wall left standing is a piece of the Western Wall. Another fact that goes unnoticed is that God will call for a sword against Gog throughout all of God's mountains.

This one simple fact shreds a very common theory. Many believe there is only one war of Gog and Magog and that it is the battle of Armageddon. There is actually a second battle of Gog and Magog after the millennial reign, but the first one is not the battle of Armageddon. This battle is a war. There is fighting, and the weapons from this war will be burned for fuel for seven years.

The battle of Armageddon isn't even a war; it's not a battle at all. It is when the Antichrist mobilizes all his troops in the plains of Megiddo and Jesus wipes them out with a spoken word or one swipe of His sword, which comes out of His mouth, suggesting He speaks. There is no one gathered to fight the army of the Antichrist. The battle of Armageddon or lack thereof is won with the return of Jesus Christ.

This battle of Gog and Magog is won in an actual battle that God contributes greatly to as well as there are still seven years or more left on earth after this war. Therefore, it cannot be the battle of

Armageddon. The battle of Gog and Magog also takes place in the valley of Jezreel, not the plains of Megiddo. Do not get these two mixed up. After this battle, the valley will be renamed the valley of Hamongog. There is so much more. Study more on this subject.

The world is preparing for this war right now. Many of the definite countries—such as Turkey, Iran, Libya, and all the terrorists groups—call for the extinction of Israel on a regular basis. If they were to ban together and march for Israel, thinking they were on their way to Mecca next, trying to bring about jihad, it would fulfill this prophecy and a few others all at the same time. When this war happens, rest assured, tribulation is right on its heels.

CHAPTER 7

What Do People Need to Know about the Tribulation?

SO WHEN DOES TRIBULATION START? What is tribulation? What event marks the beginning of the seven-year period known as Jacob's trouble? What happens to the body of Christ? There are many questions about tribulation and a lot of confusion as well. When it comes to tribulation, the great tribulation, and the rapture, there is much disagreement and division between the saints. The most important thing is that everyone acknowledges exactly what scripture says and will rely on God's Word.

Since there are a multitude of wolves in sheep's clothing out there just waiting to deceive as many as possible at the next turn, everything must be tested by the Holy Spirit. The truth is important in this hour.

No one can count on something just because the majority agree on this version or because this version sounds easier or because this is what their pastor taught them all their life, and the same goes for their mother's pastor. I don't care if that's what they teach in Bible college, if an angel came down from heaven and told them, or if they had a vision of being taken to heaven and think they spoke to God. If it isn't undoubtedly supported by scripture, it's not right and not from God.

God and Jesus are the same yesterday, today, and tomorrow. God doesn't change, and neither does His Word. Heaven and earth will pass away, but the Word of God will never pass away. There are so many deceived that need to unlearn what they have been taught no matter how wonderful it sounds because that just isn't what the Bible says. This isn't a time line of events or breakdown of instructions but more of an explanation of the purpose of tribulation, how to know when it is here, and what effects it has on the saints.

The tribulation is a seven-year period also known as Jacob's trouble. Tribulation is split into two periods of three and a half years each. All seven years are known as tribulation, but the last three and a half years are the great tribulation period. Sticking with the same metaphor that Jesus set forth, it is when the contractions get the heaviest and the most painful part of labor before the birth.

For now, this chapter will concentrate on the period as a whole and the first half. Tribulation is not God's wrath, and that is detrimental to comprehend. Though there are seven bowls/vials of wrath in the great tribulation, that doesn't constitute labeling the whole event God's wrath. God's wrath is the condemnation to the lake of fire, also known as hell, for all eternity. God's wrath is the wages of sin, which is death. When the Bible speaks of the great day of His wrath has come, it speaks to the wrath that comes at death and the day of the Lord when a person isn't born again. The day of the Lord is the last day on earth. It is judgment against a world full of iniquity but doesn't compare to His wrath.

> He that believeth on the Son hath everlasting life:
> and he that believeth not the Son shall not see
> life; but the wrath of God abideth on him. (Joel
> 3:36)

> For the wages of sin is death; but the gift of God
> is eternal life through Jesus Christ our Lord.
> (Rom. 6:23)

The tribulation is the period when the devil is cast down to earth and has only a short time left. The tribulation is the devil's wrath. It is the devil's anger at being out of time and defeated by the cross. It starts when Michael and his angels fought with Satan in the heavens and threw him down to earth along with the fallen angels

(Rev. 12:7–13). This happens in the spiritual realm. No one is going to see a big red serpent fall from the clouds and hit the ground. So how can it be known when that happens in the physical realm or natural world?

There are a few things to look for to note the beginning of the tribulation period. Daniel's definition of the start of the seventieth week or tribulation is the covenant for one week with many. When referencing this to many other scriptures, it is determined that doesn't mean a week like most see it but instead a seven-year period, with each day representing a year. A year is also referred to in the Bible as a time, which would make half a time or a divided time to be half of a year.

Now keep in mind a year isn't a year on the Gregorian calendar but instead a biblical or Hebrew year, which is 360 days. This covenant is a peace treaty signed by the Antichrist and Israel that has been reborn for the last days and has been in constant war since. It is most likely at this moment that all will know who the Antichrist is. This is the Antichrist revealed.

The beginning of tribulation will also bring another event. Though this event is not specifically defined as to whether or not it is to the day, it could be give or take a few days. The book of Revelation gives so much detail on tribulation. Revelation says that Jerusalem will be divided by introducing that the outer courts of the temple will belong to the Gentiles for forty-two months (Rev. 11:1–2). This has to be at the first half of tribulation due to the fact that the Antichrist takes control of the temple during the great tribulation. Revelation 11 continues to discuss the two witnesses. Though it doesn't say whether the two witnesses appear at the beginning of tribulation or the great tribulation, by context clues, it can be safely assumed that they do not appear until after the first half of the seven years as it is included in the second woe or sixth trumpet. That will be discussed further in the next chapter.

In Matthew, Jesus gives a warning to all who will hear. He says:

> But as the days of Noe were, so shall also the coming of the Son of man be. For as in the days that were before the flood they were eating and

drinking, marrying and giving in marriage, until
the day that Noe entered into the ark, And knew
not until the flood came, and took them all away;
so shall also the coming of the Son of man be.
(Matt. 24:37–39)

In the days of Noah, people made fun of Noah for warning
them. They called him crazy and told him there was no flood coming. They didn't care what Noah said; they wouldn't turn their faces
to the Lord. They refused to believe His messengers. In the days of
Noah, God saved His chosen people from destruction. He didn't do
this by removing them from earth but instead by giving them special
instructions. If they obeyed these instructions, they would be spared,
and if they didn't, they would die. He told Noah to get in the ark
and he will be saved. God said, "Obey my instructions, and you will
be spared." The rest of the world just kept on committing sins, con-
demning Noah for being too serious and for obeying God. As in the
days of Noah, so shall the coming of the Son of man be.

According to 2 Thessalonians at this time, when the son of perdition is revealed, because the world didn't want to have God present
to hold him back, then God will send a strong delusion to everyone
that didn't believe the truth (2 Thess. 2:6–12). He will cause them
to be damned that are not sanctified in the Spirit and believe the
truth. In other words, everyone that isn't a born-again, Spirit-filled
Christian will be deceived and will worship the Antichrist because
God Almighty will make them. Once tribulation begins, no one else
can come to the salvation of Jesus Christ.

When the Antichrist is revealed, there will be no other saints
other than what is already on earth at that moment. It means when
the Antichrist is revealed, time is up. If there is anyone that hasn't
already given their heart to Jesus, then they will never get the chance.
The hourglass will run out of sand, and the saints that go through tribulation will all be saved before it starts. This means tribulation starts
soon after the people remove God from the government, schools, the
workplace, the public in general, and yes, even the church buildings.

If a church isn't preaching true doctrine, then the Lord isn't
there. If the church is part of the world rather than separated from

it, then God isn't there. If the church has a preacher that deems sin acceptable in this day and age because of the times (such as fornication, homosexuality, transgender, abortion, or the like), then God isn't there. If God isn't there, it isn't because He abandoned the church, but because He and His Word were no longer welcome.

There is no prayer in schools, no Ten Commandments at the courthouse, and no preaching the gospel in many streets allowed because they claim it to be offensive. This world is so close to evicting God from every part of life except the few strong Christians that aren't ashamed of Jesus. Soon the only place where sound doctrine can be heard will be in makeshift churches in homes of Spirit-filled believers.

The effects of tribulation will be global, though only believers will fully comprehend what is occurring as everyone else was made to believe the lies the son of perdition spewed when Jacob's trouble started. The rest of the world just thinks everything is peachy and there is peace and safety. The Bible says, "But when they say peace and safety then sudden destruction will come upon them." The deception is supported by Revelation, which says all that are on earth whose names aren't written in the Lamb's book of life will worship the lawless one or Antichrist (Rev. 13:8). It is followed by the important words the Bible uses when it wants the people to pay attention: "If any man have ears let him hear" (Rev. 13:9).

Another effect of tribulation is the beast system rising. The preparations for the beast system can already be seen in all three factions blatantly, but the actual system will start to take hold in the beginning of tribulation. The third faction isn't fully completed until the mark of the beast during the great tribulation.

What are the three factions of the beast system? They consist of a one world government, one world religion, and one world monetary system in the form of a cashless society. The beast system's purpose is to control the people, hunt out the Christians, get as many as possible to fall away and deny Jesus or take the mark, and slaughter the rest or imprison them and make examples of them so more will fall away. The devil's time is short, so now he will attempt to take souls by the illusion of force and the usual deceptions, but those that endure to the end will be saved. Breaking down each faction of the beast system really isn't that confusing.

There will be one world government all ran by the Antichrist according to Revelation (Rev. 13:2, 7). The Antichrist will be given power by Satan over all kindred, tongues, and nations. Now there is already a global government, but right now it doesn't impede the governments of each nation unless they violate international laws or extreme moral codes if they aren't a member.

The United Nations has been preparing and indoctrinating the world for global rule for many years. Isn't it funny that they were established with the rebirth of Israel? That was no accident. Agenda 21 is also more indoctrination, getting us accustomed to the UN controlling the world and telling us what to do, eat, say, wear and where to do it and how to do it. All these factions will come under the disguise of peace, love, unity, safety, and equality.

The new Sustainable Development Agenda passed by the UN vaguely lays out goals and rules that if countries agree to give them the right to take our properties, food, belongings, freedom, children, and more and even put us in work camps all for the betterment of feeding the poor, conserving energy, etc., it could allow the government to hand out what each person needs as well as raise the children as they are "more qualified" and parents might fill their heads with things about God. This has been setting up for a very long time, guys. President Obama is definitely a preparation tool and an Antichrist spirit, but he is not the cause of all this. Look at the puppet master, not the puppet.

The one world religion will rear its ugly head by starting as all religions uniting in peace. This religion is laid out in Revelation (Rev. 13:4, 8). The world is already preparing for this as the pope and people everywhere are calling for everyone to unite in peace, respecting all religions. There are people saying there are many ways to get to heaven, and of course, don't forget the coexist movement with all the religious symbols inside the letters of the word *coexist*.

Then at the start of the great tribulation, it will be declared that everyone must worship the Antichrist. He will tell everyone he is God. That will be broken down a bit more in the next chapter also.

He will have helpers performing false miracles in his name. All that don't belong to Jesus will worship him. All that don't worship him will be beheaded or killed. Everyone will be told to get a mark that proves it. On the last day, every person will have a seal—either the seal of God or the mark of the beast.

The mark of the beast is the ultimate goal for a one world currency or monetary system that is a cashless society. It has already started as well. Most don't even realize the subtle changes in their lifestyle. The world started out using cash and goods. Period. Cash could be paper, coins, gold, silver, or any form but money. Then checks were introduced—not a big change. Checks are about the same size as paper money and are still paper, but they got everyone prepared to use debit and credit cards, and wiring money prepared the people for electronic transfers.

All these prepared the world for chips in their credit cards that can track you, which they claim is safer, and for paying for things through apps, PayPal, Bitcoin, etc. These all allow them to know what a person bought, how many, when, how often, and more. All these things transitioned everyone into things like Apple Pay, or Wal-Mart Pay, and other similarities that use a phone to purchase things.

Now they have Apple watches and other brands that place the phone on the wrist. Where do most people wear a watch? The majority wear them on the right hand. They are developing technology that allows a bracelet to project a phone directly onto the arm. This currently is indoctrinating people to swipe their hand to pay for things.

Computers are now getting the ability to use fingerprints and scans of the faces to log in. Biometrics is becoming highly popular, and Google is developing a chip that goes in the eye. Slowly they are getting the masses accustomed to paying for goods by the head or hand. What will the mark of the beast be? Where will it be? It will be placed IN, not on, the right hand or forehead. It could be a chip or an electronic tattoo or something else similar.

It will need to store large amounts of information electronically and in a tiny size. The doctors are pushing for chips in the hand for all the medical records of a person. They are already using chips in the hand to clock in at work, unlock doors, show identification, get into soccer games, provide security clearance, and much more. Very soon, those little RFID chips will hold everything, and most will transition very easily because it is so easy, safe, and convenient. They won't even realize what they are doing. Revelation describes the money system and the mark of the beast (Rev. 13:16–18). It will be stated that if someone doesn't get the chip, then they can't buy or sell anything because it will all be done on credit and cash won't exist. This is another way to ensure more Christians die due to starvation or denounce Christ so they or their families can eat.

There will be a very important player pushing all these agendas that rise with the beast system. Revelation shows the false prophet stepping on the scene (Rev. 13:11–14). He witnesses that the Antichrist should be worshiped and forces people to bow to his image. He performs false miracles and brings fire from the sky. The beast system, Antichrist, and false prophet will cause many to fall away if the saints aren't ready in faith and didn't obey God like Noah did. Those that didn't get in the ark at all, meaning covered in the blood of Jesus, will be condemned to the lake of fire because after three and a half years of rough tribulation comes the great tribulation. This will hold so much peril for those in Christ, the fulfillment of the mark of the beast, the persecution of the saints, and so much more.

CHAPTER 8

What Do People Need to Know about the Great Tribulation?

HALFWAY INTO THE TRIBULATION, THERE will be a period called the great tribulation. It is the last three and a half years of the seven-year tribulation period. It is called the great tribulation for multiple reasons, but this reference is used mainly because even Jesus refers to it as such. In Matthew, Jesus says, "For then shall be great tribulation" (Matt. 24:21). How is it known He is speaking of this time period and not the seven years as a whole? What exactly is the difference between the great tribulation and the rest of the tribulation period? How will everyone know precisely when it starts? What happens to the saints during this time? In this chapter, these questions will be answered.

The great tribulation is the absolute worst time this world will ever see. There has never been and will never be anything worse than what will happen during this sequence of events. It will be worse than any horror movie ever seen for those that are not in the ark, which is covered in blood of Jesus. Those that are in the ark will still see persecution as the Antichrist makes war with the saints. The born-again Christians have one duty during this time, and only one; endure. They must endure in love, endure in sound doctrine, endure in faith and courage, and most importantly, endure in the acknowledgment of the belief in the gospel of Jesus Christ. The worst thing that a Christian can do throughout this is deny Jesus or take the mark of the beast in order to escape death. It will be a period of great sorrow and trials. Stand fast to the Lord.

The great tribulation begins with the abomination that causes desolation. This is defined by Daniel (Dan. 11:30–39). This is when the Antichrist takes over Jerusalem; sits in the temple, declaring himself to be God; and takes away the daily sacrifice. He will claim to be the only god and above all others. He will claim he is the only one that has heard everyone's prayers. He will speak great blasphemies on the God of Israel, Abraham, Isaac, and Jacob. It is also mentioned in the book of Daniel; Daniel tells us it is in the middle of the seven years that this occurs (Dan. 9:26–27). This time frame and events are supported in Revelation, and it is also confirmed that it happens in the temple in 2 Thessalonians (Rev. 13:5–6; 2 Thess. 2:4). After this, he declares war on the saints. This is explained further in Daniel and many other places (Dan. 11:30–39). This is the beginning of the final persecutions and the worst of them all.

What is the difference in the first half of tribulation and the great tribulation? In the first half of Jacob's trouble, the Antichrist holds to the treaty of peace. He will do things here and there that are unthinkable, but it won't be until after he takes Jerusalem that he truly rules the world with an iron fist. At first, he will use persuasion and excuses, but then he will use blunt force and dictator tactics, and the deceived will follow and cheer. The acts carried out after the abomination won't just be unthinkable but will be horrific and unimaginable. The great tribulation will truly fit the meaning of Satan's wrath.

Next turn back to Matthew, and notice that Jesus said, "When you see the abomination that causes desolation spoken of in Daniel" (Matt. 24:15–21). He didn't say, "When the treaty is signed." He noted the specific event of the abomination in the holy place. That's because it was bad before, but it was nothing compared to what is coming next. He says, "When you see this, those that are in Judaea, run!" Don't stop to get clothes, pack a bag, or anything else. Just run. Run and hide in the mountains. Pray that you aren't pregnant or nursing in that day and that it isn't winter or Sabbath when the time comes. Note what He says (Matt. 24:21). He gives everyone the "when" first and then what to do, followed by why. He says when you see the abomination that causes desolation (Matt. 24:15), flee (Matt. 24:16) because then shall be great tribulation (Matt. 24:21). He plainly tells the world nothing has ever been or will ever be this bad again. It is so horrific that if He doesn't intervene and shorten it, there wouldn't be anyone left alive. Jesus states clearly this is the signal of the beginning of the great tribulation. This is how everyone can know which time period He speaks of when He names the great tribulation. It starts when the abomination that causes desolation stands in the temple. This is the last half of the seven-year period. This is also supported by Mark (Mark 13:14–19).

Sometime just before the start of the great tribulation or soon after it, the two witnesses should appear. The timing of the two witnesses isn't completely definitive according to scripture. It is known by scripture for certain that they will be here for 1,260 days. It is assumed the timing will be around the great tribulation because their death occurs during the second woe or sixth trumpet. Jesus returns at the seventh trumpet at the end of the great tribulation.

As Revelation reads, the two witnesses are introduced in Jerusalem (Rev. 11). The world will know it is the two witnesses because they will come preaching the law, and if anyone tries to harm them, fire will come out of their mouth and devour the enemy. Revelation says this is how that person must die (Rev. 11:5).

It goes on to say that these two can cause droughts, turn water to blood, bring about plagues, and such as often as they want while they are prophesying. After they prophesy for 1,260 days, the Antichrist will kill them and leave them lying in the streets. No one will move them or try to bury them for three and a half days. The world will celebrate over their deaths and send gifts to one another. Three and a half days will pass, and the Spirit of God will enter them, and they will stand up, which causes the world to fear. Then God calls to them and raises them to heaven while their enemies watch. This will be followed by a great earthquake that causes a tenth of the city to fall, killing seven thousand men or people (Rev. 11).

What happens to the saints during this time period? The warning from our Savior tells those in Judea to flee to the mountains. This could mean those that actually live in the territory of Judea, but I doubt that if Jesus was speaking of the natural realm, only the people in that state would be in danger. Would those in Israel as a whole not be in danger? What if by Judea He were speaking symbolically of those that are in Christ?

Here is the breakdown of this logic. Jesus is the Lion of Judah, coming from the tribe of Judah. Judea is the name of the land that belonged to the tribe of Judah. If someone has been redeemed by the blood of Christ, then they are in the body of Christ or in Christ. If they are in Christ, it can be said they are in the Lion of Judah and thus the tribe of Judah. Whatever land the Lord has given this person belongs to Judah; therefore, it is Judea. This very well could be a warning to all those in Christ.

With that said, does that mean run and hide in the mountains? Psalms says God is our refuge, our rock, and our fortress (Psalm 91). Many times the Bible refers to the holy mountain in referring to His temple. Where is His temple now in the new covenant? His temple is the body of every saint, and Jesus is the rock. Therefore, as a matter of opinion, this means the saints must hide and take refuge in Jesus. Jesus is the ark, the mountain, the rock, and the only escape.

This doesn't mean any person will be protected from persecution. Every person that takes refuge in the rock will be protected from the seals, trumpets, bowls of wrath, but not from persecution. Jesus said, "Take up your cross and follow me," not "sit this one out." The Bible says all who believe in Christ will suffer persecution. This doesn't mean every person will die, but they will suffer some form of persecution. Even being made fun of for continued faith is persecution. However, in the great tribulation, persecution is defined.

It can be seen that the saints will be overcome, referring back to Revelation (Rev. 13:7–10). It says the false prophet makes an image of the beast or Antichrist and gives it life in Revelation (Rev. 13:14–15). This image can speak, and it orders everyone to worship the image. If someone refuses, then they will be put to death. Everyone that refuses to bow to the Antichrist or his image receives a death sentence.

Then the order is given for the mark of the beast. The only way someone can buy or sell anything is by taking this mark (Rev. 13:16–18). Those that aren't prepared will most likely starve to death. This is one way that Jesus means we must endure to the end. This mark will be something that goes in, not on, the right hand or the forehead. At no time before now has the technology been present to have an image of a beast that spoke and have something that could be placed in the skin that could allow the people to buy and sell anything.

Artificial intelligence, holograms, RFID chips, and microchip technology can complete all this without anything out of the ordinary. There are also tattoos that can include electronic circuitry now that could be used as well. Google already wants to put a chip in the eye. The rest has already been addressed as far as biometrics, medical record chips, and other areas previously mentioned. Those that are caught without the mark will be beheaded.

How can that be known? All that do not worship the Antichrist and his image get a death sentence. If someone won't take the mark, they obviously don't worship him. Revelation says John saw the souls of those that were beheaded for Christ, those that had not worshiped the beast or his image or taken the mark of the beast (Rev. 20:4). Those that stand true to Christ will be beheaded. Prepare for this mentally, in faith, emotionally, and do not deny Jesus when the time comes.

Those that endure through this will reign with Jesus for a thousand years. It is worth it. Endure! He died on the cross for the world, and it was not quick. This is the least the last generation can do for Him. With all this said, there are many feeling scared and confused right now. Anyone that has surrendered their heart to Jesus has no need to fear a thing. Trust God. If there is someone reading that hasn't repented and let Jesus change their life and are obeying God's commandments, then it is strongly urged they follow all the instructions in the next chapter before it is too late. They definitely have a reason to be very afraid.

CHAPTER 9

How Can Saints Be Prepared?

IT TAKES A MULTIPLE LAYER of areas to be prepared and protected for tribulation, rapture, and the day of the Lord. In this chapter, the discussion will keep to the preparation of the inside: the spirit, heart, mind, and faith. The Bible explains in detail where everyone's walk with Christ should be in order to be ready.

First and most importantly, it is detrimental and urgent that each person be in the ark. What does this mean? Just as in the days of Noah, in order to be saved, Noah and his family had to actually enter the ark and obey God's instructions, or they would have died along with everyone else.

Today the instructions given to the world are not to build a giant ark. The ark that must be entered now is a different one, a symbolic ark. To be in the ark now, one must be covered in the blood of Jesus, be a born-again Christian. In order to be safe, a person must have surrendered their heart, soul, mind, body, and their entire life to Jesus and put it in His control. There is much scripture to support this.

One very important passage to calm fear and remind the people of His promise is Psalm 91. It promises that if a person is saved and born again, then they are in the secret place of the Most High. This puts them in the shadow of the Almighty. He is the refuge or fortress that the saints can trust for safety. Psalm 91 states that He will deliver His saints from the snares and pestilence. He will cover them, and they will use His wings as their shield. There is no need to be afraid of any terror, arrows, other forms of attacks, pestilence, or destruction.

It promises to the saints that a thousand will fall at their side and ten thousand at their right hand, but it won't come near them because they will only see the reward of the wicked with their eyes.

When a saint lives in Jesus, they live in a fortress of protection, and no evil will befall them, nor will any plague come near their house. His angels are sent to protect every saint, to keep watch over all of God's children, and to keep them from harm. Because of this, they will trample the enemies. God's love is upon them, and they will be delivered in times of trouble because they know Jesus and praise His name (Ps. 91). He will never leave their side and will show them salvation. This is an all-encompassing statement and promise of the Lord's protection.

Then there is Psalm 23, which commands the saints not to be afraid because God walks with them and shows them the ways He is with them. Jesus is the Great Shepherd and provides for His flock. He gives the flock rest, leads them to peaceful waters, restores their soul, and shows the way of righteousness. It doesn't matter if the flock is facing death. He is there, and they should fear no evil (Ps. 23).

God's children can't be defeated even in death. They can't be killed because they have eternity in Christ. They will be resurrected on the last day. The flocks are anointed children of God, comforted by His rod and staff, and will be sat at a table before their enemies. They will dwell in the house of the Lord forever, and goodness and mercy will follow them wherever they go.

Isaiah shows more promises that can be declared over a saint's life. Isaiah declares that by Jesus's stripes, those washed in the blood of Jesus are healed (Isa. 53:5). Jesus paid for the healing of the saints as well as their salvation on the cross. It just requires going to battle using the Word of God and faith to invoke it.

Isaiah has another proclamation that can be used and a promise to His children. It states no weapon formed against a saint will prosper and that every tongue that rises against them in judgment will be condemned (Isa. 54:17). This is the heritage of the servants of the Lord, and their righteousness is of the Lord.

When a person becomes born again, the Holy Spirit comes to live in them, and they receive the armor of God. This armor is a protection against the devil, his demons, and any attacks the enemy can throw as long as the saints use their armor. It is discussed and described in Ephesians (Eph. 6:11–17). The saint's battle isn't against flesh and blood but instead against principalities and powers like the demons, fallen angels, and Satan.

When the children of God put on their armor and keep it on, they are protected, able to withstand the evil day, having done all to stand. The evil day is another way to say the coming day of the Lord and also the attacks that are received until that day. What is the armor of God?

The armor consists of certain attributes. The loins are girted with truth. This means a saint must study the Word of God and know truth—not just what Bible colleges or their pastor taught them, but truth taught by the Holy Spirit Himself. It means the Word must be rightly divided and not twisted to make it mean what someone wants it to mean or to agree with what they were already taught. Sometimes this means unlearning things they thought they knew all their life.

The breastplate is made of righteousness. No person has righteousness, but it is instead obtained when they are washed clean of their sin by the blood of Jesus and then go and live holy lives as commanded by the Bible. This doesn't mean they are perfect but that when they make a mistake, they repent and change their ways. Every day they grow in Christ and therefore maintain their righteousness and clean garments. The feet are shod with the preparation of the gospel of peace. This is the gospel of Jesus Christ, His love and salvation and call to repentance, which brings every saint peace.

The shield is an undying faith in His promises, the Word of God, the finished work of the cross, and His will being what's best above their own desires and wants. It allows the saints to deflect the fiery darts the enemy throws to attack them in the spiritual realm. The helmet is the salvation of Jesus Christ and the acceptance of His death, resurrection, and sacrifice to pay for the sins of everyone. It doesn't just mean saying a little prayer and then going about their business but allowing that prayer and Jesus to change their lives through obedience and walking the narrow path.

Then there is the weapon each saint is given. The sword, the Word of God, is the greatest weapon one can take up. Simply speaking the Word of God is a powerful attack in spiritual warfare (Eph. 6:11–17). God spoke this world into creation. It was His Word that created everything. That Word then became flesh as His Son, Jesus, who died to save all of mankind that will choose to follow Jesus.

When it is all over, Jesus will destroy the armies of the Antichrist with the Word. He will simply speak, and the armies will be slaughtered. The Word of God is the most powerful thing that has ever or will ever exist. These pieces are combined with prayer and supplication in the Spirit.

Praying in the Spirit requires a prayer language or speaking in tongues. This is supported in Ephesians as well when it says that "utterance may be given to me" (Eph. 6:19). That is cross-referenced with Acts, which says, "When they were filled with the Holy Ghost, the Spirit gave them utterance, and they spoke in other tongues" (Acts 2:4). It shows that utterance means speaking in tongues. Speaking in tongues is part of the armor of God. Those that wear the armor are prepared for battle.

If a soldier is prepared for battle, then they can walk in the power and authority that is given to every believer in Christ. Luke shows how Jesus gives every believer power over serpents and scorpions, which are demons, and other principalities and over all the power of the enemy (Luke 10:19). Then He promises that nothing shall by any means hurt you. This means that power can be used to defend any saint and keep them from harm and nothing the devil or his friends throw at them can hurt them.

The saints are commanded to speak the gospels and not to be afraid. As a matter of fact, the Bible commands the people 365 times not to be afraid. Acts 18:9–10 is one such command, telling the saints not to be quiet or hold their peace but to proclaim God's Word no matter what because they are protected.

There are many saying right now that just because a saint is protected doesn't mean they can't die. They are afraid of death or giving their life for Christ. Guess what, anyone that is born again can't be killed. How is that? It's because they are already dead. A born-again Christian died the minute they gave their life to Jesus. They died, and it is Jesus that lives in them. Someone that is already dead can't be killed. They will spend eternity with Christ and be resurrected on the last day. The worst that can happen is they get to sleep for a little while. Yes, the fleshly body will be dead, but they will get a new one, a spiritual body. They were crucified with Christ; therefore, they are already dead, and it is Christ Jesus that lives in their place (Gal. 2:20).

There are many verses that show what protection is given and support the points made when a person is in Christ. John tells the saints they aren't of the world that will suffer tribulation and Jesus has already overcome the world (John 16:33; John 17:15–16). The saints can't be separated from the love of God. They can backslide and refuse His love, but that is another matter. That love rests in Jesus, who gives every saint His protection (Rom. 8:31). Believers are delivered from wicked men and evil, and this can be read in 2 Thessalonians (2 Thess. 3:2–3).

The most important thing to do to be prepared for the last days is for each person to surrender their life to Jesus, repent of their sins, obey God's commandments (which are the Bible), and be born again and baptized in the Holy Spirit. Yes, there is a difference between the Holy Spirit coming into a person's heart when they are saved and the baptism of the Holy Spirit.

When a person is saved, the Holy Spirit goes into their heart. When a person is baptized in the Holy Spirit, it overflows out of their heart and completely engulfs them like water. This is why it is called the baptism or infilling of the Holy Spirit. When someone is baptized in water, they are entirely engulfed in water. The baptism of the Holy Spirit brings the gifts of the Holy Spirit as listed and explained in 1 Corinthians 12. These gifts edify the saints and help them to do God's work as He has planned.

The first 120 received the Holy Ghost on the day of Pentecost, 50 days after the Resurrection in Acts (Acts 2:1–4). They began to speak in tongues. Acts told them it was coming (Acts 1:5) and relayed that it would give them power or authority in Jesus (Acts 1:8). Peter announced to the Jews that everyone must repent and be baptized in the name of Jesus for the remission of sins and receive the Holy Ghost (Acts 2:38). Jesus said in Acts that "John baptized in water, but ye shall be baptized with the Holy Ghost" (Acts 11:16). The Holy Ghost is power from on high according to Luke (Luke 24:49).

It says in John that John the Baptist knew while Jesus was still alive that it would be Him who would baptize people in the Holy Spirit by the fact that the dove descended from heaven when John baptized Jesus in water (John 1:33). Only those that are born again can receive the Holy Spirit. The world cannot because they don't know Jesus. The Holy Spirit never leaves and is a Comforter, Teacher, Counselor, and much more (John 14:16–17, 26). The Holy Spirit shows the person truth, which is part of the armor of God (John 16:13).

The Holy Spirit is a freely given gift of the Lord but must be received. It can be blocked or refused like any gift. Doubt, fear, unbelief, failure to renounce things like witchcraft or satanic worship or failure to trust in God can block the gift of the Holy Spirit. Not everyone is ready to walk in the power that comes with it. A person must willingly accept it and not doubt its existence or power.

After a person receives the gift, they can do great things in the name of Jesus. They can cast out demons, lays hands on people and heal, speak and pray in tongues, prophesy, and other things. Each person can have different gifts and may not have all the gifts. All these things are done in Jesus's name to glorify Him because the Holy Spirit is given by Him. The apostles received it directly from Jesus before the Ascension, but it didn't manifest until the day of Pentecost because that was the day appointed. Jesus breathed on them and told them to receive the Holy Spirit (John 20:21–22).

If there is anyone that needs help becoming born again or baptized in the Holy Spirit, please see the back of the book. I urge everyone that isn't saved to accept Jesus as their Savior, to repent of their sins, and to receive the baptism of the Holy Spirit. Once this is done, there is nothing to fear. There will be peace available in faith that is undefinable, and they will be under the protection of the Most High God.

Once someone is baptized in the Spirit, they will produce good fruit. Every born-again Christian is a branch of the True Vine, which is Jesus Christ, as mentioned in John. If they do not bear good fruit, they will be removed and cast into the fire (John 15:1–2). If they abide in Jesus, they will bear good fruit, and if they do not, they won't. No one can bear fruit of the Spirit without being in Jesus, says John (John 15:4–6). The Holy Spirit is a testimony of Jesus, and so is the fruit of the Spirit. Those that are ordained by Jesus will bring forth good fruit, and whatever they ask in Jesus's name will be done (John 15:16, 26). The fruit of the Spirit is listed in Galatians (Gal. 5:22–23). It is love, peace, joy, long-suffering, gentleness, goodness, faith, meekness, and temperance or self-control. Even Romans says that the saints are dead to the law by the body of Christ, married to one another and Christ that we should bring forth good fruit (Rom. 7:4).

In order to bring forth good fruit, one must walk in the Spirit and deny the flesh. Except a man be born of water and Spirit, he cannot enter the kingdom of God (John 3:5–6). That which is born of flesh is flesh, and that which is born of Spirit is spirit. When a person walks in the Spirit, they know the voice of the Lord. They have a personal relationship with Him. Jesus goes before them, and they follow Him and hear His voice (John 10:4, 27).

There are many great Bible studies available on walking in the Spirit. A great one by evangelist Anita Fuentes is quoted saying, "To walk in the Spirit means to be led by the Spirit. To be led by the Spirit means to live according to the Spirit. To live according to the Spirit means to be spiritually minded." It is based off Galatians 5:16–20 (Fuentes, "EMOAF Biblical Session 2, Course 12").

How does someone know if they are acting in the manner they are supposed to other than bearing good fruit? How does one walk in the Spirit? There are many instructions in scripture as to how to behave and be spiritually minded. If the saints walk in the Spirit and not in the flesh, there is no more condemnation for them because the law of the Spirit and life makes them free from the law of sin and death. They are still bound by law, just not the same law.

Now they are bound by the law of the Spirit, which means they are to walk in the Spirit, as it states in Romans (Rom. 8:1–2). Romans states righteousness of the law is only fulfilled by walking in the Spirit. Those that walk in the Spirit do things of the Spirit, unlike those that walk in flesh. To walk in the flesh or be carnally minded and obey desires is death. To be spiritually minded is life and peace. This is because the carnal mind is enmity against God as it is not subject to the law of God or can be. If someone is walking in the flesh, then they can't make God happy (Rom. 8:4–14).

If the Spirit of God dwells in someone, they are not in the flesh, but if they don't have the Spirit of Christ, then they are not Christ's. If Christ is in that person, then their body is dead because of sin, and the Spirit is life because of righteousness. The Holy Spirit will also quicken their mortal bodies. Those that walk in the Spirit and are led by the Spirit are the sons of God, His children.

Those that walk in the Spirit will let love be without suppression, hate evil, be affectionate to each other in brotherly love, fervent in spirit, not lazy in business, serve the Lord, rejoice in hope, and patient in tribulation; and continuing instant in prayer. They will be given to hospitality, distributing to the needs of the saints, and will bless those that persecute them, not place curses. They will rejoice with those that rejoice, weep with those that weep, and be of the same mind toward one another. They will not want high things, not look down on those less fortunate or of lower position, not take revenge. They will be humble, be honest, be peaceful, not be vengeful, and they will feed the poor. They will owe no man anything and will love one another. They will not commit adultery, not kill, not steal, not bear false witness, not covet, and they will love their neighbor (Rom. 12:9–21; Rom. 13:8–10).

Ephesians says to walk with lowliness, meekness, long-suffering, forgiving one another in love and endeavoring to keep the unity of the Spirit in the bond of peace (Eph. 4:1–4). Ephesians also has guidelines for walking in the Spirit. Those that are spiritually minded will put away lying and speak truth, not sin when they are angry, not let the sun go down on their wrath, not give place to the devil. They will work so that they have something to give to the needy. They will not let corrupt communication proceed out of their mouth but only that which is good for edifying, not grieving, the Holy Spirit. They will put away all bitterness, wrath, anger, clamor, evil speaking, and malice, and they will be kind to one another, be tenderhearted, and forgiving. They will walk in love and not let fornication, unclean- ness, filthiness, foolish talking, jesting, or covetousness be named among them. They will not be deceived by vain words, not be a whoremonger, not be an idolater, and have no fellowship with the works of darkness but instead scold them. They will walk as children of the light and will understand what the will of the Lord is. They will not be drunk but will be filled with the Spirit, speaking psalms and hymns and spiritual songs, and they will give thanks to the Lord for all things in the name of Jesus (Eph. 4:25–32; Eph. 5:1–21).

Philippians says they will do all things without murmurings or dispute and will hold forth the word of life. They should also know which people labor in Christ among them and esteem them highly and be at peace among one another. They will warn those that are unruly, comfort the feeble-minded, support the weak, be patient toward all men, see that no one takes revenge, follow that which is good, rejoice evermore, pray without ceasing, not quench the Spirit, not despise prophecies or those that give them, prove all things, and abstain from the appearance of evil (Phil. 2:14–16). In 1 John, it informs the saints that the lust of the flesh, lust of the eyes, and the pride of life are of the world and not of the Father (1 John 2:16). All these things are behaviors that those who walk in the Spirit should have. "Open Your Eyes People with Evangelist Anita Fuentes" has complete and thorough classes on the subject (Fuentes, "EMOAF Bible Session 2, Course 12").

In order to be spiritually prepared for the things that are coming, everyone must be a born-again Christian that has surrendered their life to Jesus and follows His commandments. They need to be bap- tized in the Holy Spirit in order to receive instructions in the Spirit so that they may pray in tongues and have their spirit speak directly to the Lord even when they don't know what to pray for. These instruc- tions, comforts, and sources of strength will be vital. Walking in the

Spirit refills the oil in the lamps, as spoken of in Matthew 25. It readies each person's faith and fulfills God's will. These three things will leave a person spiritually ready to enter the times ahead.

CHAPTER 10

What Responsibilities and Physical Preparations Are Necessary?

ALONG WITH SPIRITUAL PREPARATION, THERE are many physical preparations that can be made as well as certain responsibilities God's children will have in these last days. The consequences of not sticking to the responsibilities given to each saint can range from bad to dire. The physical preparations can be endless depending on the resources a person has, but that extent isn't exactly necessary. In each area what a person does or doesn't do could affect something as menial as comfort or as damaging as costing lives or even souls.

Starting with the responsibilities is probably the best way to go here. Every saint has responsibilities in the body of Christ on a daily basis. Each person has a different job in the body of Christ. Some are teachers, some ministers or pastors, some healers, some prophets, some watchman, some in deliverance ministry, and so on.

There are some that believe that spreading the gospel is only the job of the pastor, preacher, minister, or other leaders in the church. This couldn't be farther from the truth. It is the responsibility of every single Christian to spread the Word and good news of Jesus Christ. The Bible tells everyone to preach the Word in season and out of season and make full proof of their ministry. This is the most important job there is (2 Tim. 4:2).

Another obligation that is extremely important in these last days comes as a surprise to some because somewhere they have been taught that these things don't apply anymore. This is one of the dangers of false prophets, taking the Bible out of context, not studying the Word for themselves, and twisting scripture to agree with an idea a person wants to believe. It is absolutely necessary that Christians listen to the prophets of God, the watchmen on the wall that God has called, and the previous prophecies laid out in the Bible. It is also important that God's instructions given through the Holy Spirit are obeyed explicitly. Walk by faith, not by sight.

That doesn't mean you should do everything anyone tells you to do. Believe not every spirit but try the spirits whether they are of God because many false prophets have gone out into the world (1 John 4:1). For example, if someone approaches and tells the crowd that Jesus has returned and He is teaching in Times Square, they are not of God.

How can someone tell? If anyone tells someone something that goes against the Word of God, the Bible, they are lying. God will never send anyone to say the opposite of the Word He has already placed here. What if it doesn't go against the Bible? First and foremost, go to the Lord in prayer and ask Him; listen to His answer. Also, consider the source. Do they show the fruit of the Spirit? Judge them by their fruit. Does this make them very fearful? Does it glorify them or the Lord? Everything should glorify God. Use the discernment God gives everyone that belongs to Him.

This will require knowing the Bible, having a personal relationship with Jesus, and knowing His voice when He speaks. This comes with following the narrow path and walking in the Spirit. When someone has determined that the Lord is speaking to them through a prophet, they should obey. For example, everyone is having a lovely church service and someone stands and starts speaking in tongues. No one in the church has ever done that before, but another person just starts interpreting what they are saying. These are gifts of the Holy Spirit. If this church welcomes the Holy Spirit and isn't of the world but truly holds to the Word of God, then God is speaking. There will usually be confirmation of whatever is said. Someone else may stand up and say, "I had a dream last night that said the very same thing." The congregation should pray and ask for confirmation that this is from the Lord. If they get it, it doesn't matter if the instructions were "Everyone, leave the city tonight." They should be followed. Sometimes God warns His people in order to protect them.

There could be a bad earthquake at four in the morning. Usually, the instructions aren't that severe, but there is no telling when it comes to tribulation. Some have gotten instructions to stop walking, walk to the nearest person, and tell them Jesus loves them, while others have a dream telling them exactly which demons a loved one is fighting with. The Holy Spirit will use multiple ways to warn the people and keep His children from harm during the horrific catastrophes that will occur in the tribulation period.

Think of Noah and the instructions he received in Genesis (Gen. 6:13–22; Gen. 7:1–5). How crazy must it have seemed to him to be told to build a giant ark for eight people! Obedience of God's instructions will be highly important. If the Lord is laying on someone's heart and sending confirmation after confirmation, heed the warning.

Maybe it's "Don't take that job," "Move to this city," "Take this person to church this week," "Go stand on the corner and preach the gospel on this day at this time," or something else. Whatever it is, God knows its purpose. Preaching on that corner could be the only chance someone has to hear the gospel and surrender their life to God. There could have been a terrorist attack at the building where the new job was located. People don't know what is ahead exactly, but God does.

Trust Him, His messengers, and trust His prophets and watchman. They are only following the instructions they received no matter how crazy it makes them look. A prophet or watchman simply warns of coming danger. They are sounding a trumpet in hopes the people will hear and be saved, as written in Ezekiel (Ezek. 33:1–5; 3:1–5, 11, 17–19). Always make sure they are sent by the Lord, and then listen intently. Take everything that is heard straight to the Lord in prayer.

There are many examples and commands that concern obedience, prophets, and God instructing people in order to save them. God saved Lot in Genesis by instructing them to move out of town immediately, and it was obedience that caused them to live (Gen.

19:13–26). Those that didn't obey to every specific detail were lost. When God says, "Don't look back," He means it.

God commands the people to believe in and heed the prophets in 2 Chronicles (2 Chron. 20:20). In Daniel, he speaks a prayer for the people of Israel (Dan. 9:9–10). They are currently slaves because they didn't heed the words of the prophets when they said to obey His laws or that destruction and judgment were coming. Jeremiah commands His people to obey His voice and walk in the ways He has commanded (Jer. 7:23). The warning to heed His watchman and His words comes in Jeremiah (Jer. 6:17–19). His watchman and prophets are sent for a reason even today. These servants weren't just for the days of old.

Nowhere in the Bible does it say God will ever cease anything. Dreams, visions, prophets, watchmen, healings, miracles, speaking in tongues, casting out demons—all of it is still present to this day. God doesn't change. He is the same yesterday, today, and tomorrow. Jeremiah pleads with the people, including today, to obey the voice of the Lord again (Jer. 38:20). In 1 Samuel, it is stated that to obey the voice of the Lord is better than sacrifice (1 Sam. 15:22).

Amos explains that God won't do anything without revealing it to His prophets (Amos 3:7). Romans even says in the New Testament that not all have obeyed the gospel and believed the report (Rom. 10:16–17). It reminds faith comes by hearing and hearing by the Word of God. Those that have the power of Jesus, according to the gospel and the preaching of Jesus, that have been made manifest and by the scriptures of the prophets are made known to all nations for obedience (Rom. 16:25–26).

The weapons of spiritual warfare are used to pull down strongholds, cast down imaginations and every high thing that exalts itself above God, and bring into captivity every thought to the obedience of Christ according to 2 Corinthians (2 Cor. 10:4–5). Every single thought is to be obedient, not just actions. The scripture commands everyone not to despise "prophesyings" (1 Thess. 5:20). It is even classified as how to be spiritually minded or walk in the Spirit. Peter greets his audience with a reminder of obedience to Jesus (1 Pet. 1:2).

There are so many verses that remind us to obey God's voice. God's voice comes in many forms. He may speak directly to someone. He could choose to send them a dream or vision or revelation in the Word. He may use prophets, watchmen, or other servants obeying when they hear His voice to speak. However He chooses to speak, it is imperative that the people listen and obey.

Another thing that must be seen to is building faith and a strong relationship with Jesus. The stronger each person's faith is, the more powerful and ready they are. Next to being saved and walking in the Spirit—and this is probably the next most important item—is that everyone's faith needs to be unshakeable. It must be strong enough for us to look death in the face and not deny Jesus. This will include for individual threats as well as those pertaining to the believer's loved ones.

This is the time to sit down and have a family discussion. The whole family needs to be aware of what to expect according to the Bible. Revelation says those that stand for Jesus will be beheaded. Those that refuse the mark will be put to death. There needs to be an understanding. No matter what happens, no matter how scary, don't deny Jesus.

Children that can understand need to be told as much as possible for their age. Use parental judgment. Is everyone prepared to split up or watch the others pass? Talk to one another. Have a real, honest, emotional conversation. Relate that those in Christ have no reason to be afraid of anything. Make sure that everyone knows that when all is said and done, the final meet-up place is at heaven's gates. Death can be a scary thought, but when it is just a change of address and the new place is walking streets of gold next to Jesus, where nothing bad will ever happen to anyone ever again, it is worth it.

With a person's faith, relationship with Christ, and loved ones prepared, and with Jesus never leaving the side of any of His servants, it won't be as hard to withstand the coming persecution and being bold for the Lord. The Holy Spirit will give direction and help each person to testify and glorify Jesus right up until the last day when the last trumpet sounds. With the proper measures, the saints will endure. They will stand strong, having done all to stand, and will boldly proclaim Jesus Christ the Lord and Savior until after every knee bows to the glory and power of the King of kings. When Christ returns to take His saints home, what a glorious day that will be!

Until that day comes, each Christian must ensure that they are not part of the world. They are called to come out of the world. If they belonged to the world, the world would love each one, but the saints belong to Jesus, and just as the world hated Him, it hates the saints as well. Stay away from worldly things that influence and tempt into sin, such as music, television, and other forms of entertainment that celebrate sin. Keep away from the works of darkness, and be bold enough to call out sin and minister the consequences of it. Don't wait for people to come to church. The church is supposed to go to them. Don't keep God in the church building. Take Him everywhere, and show Him off. Advertise Him, and spread His Word everywhere. Don't be a part-timer because God wants full custody.

There is a daily battle in the spiritual realm. Spiritual warfare is very real and very much an ongoing thing. The battle is between the enemy and the children of God led by Jesus. What people need to realize is that the battle has already been won. It was won that day on the cross. Every born-again Christian has power and authority in Jesus and should understand that they are soldiers of God (Luke 10:19).

Each believer should know their authority and who they are in Christ. They should understand that those that have been baptized in the Holy Spirit and washed in the blood of the Lamb can simply command an attack to stop or a demon to leave. Demons and the fiery darts they throw are real and serious. Study the Word and go to battle daily with every weapon available. The weapons are the Word of God, which is the sword, prayer, and more. Simply reading scripture out loud and declaring it over lives is a powerful form of warfare. This is also why a healthy prayer life is imperative.

Starting the day in prayer sends a message to the enemy and cancels any plans that are already in motion as long as that's what is asked for. Prayer, worship, praising the Lord, and reading God's Word are the best weapons to fight this battle. It is highly encouraged that each believer look into some information on how to engage in spiritual warfare and what the power and authority of each Christian is (Mark 16:15–18; Luke 10:19; 2 Tim. 2:3–5; Eph. 6:10–19; Acts 19:1–18). Everyone should really dive into the subject heavily. Saints are the Lord's army. As the song says. "Onward Christian soldiers." Don't be defenseless.

Being ready for tribulation and daily battles requires spiritual strengthening and workout so to speak. This comes from praying without ceasing and fasting to build faith and a relationship with God. Fasting denies the flesh and lets the person concentrate on their walk in the Spirit. It allows a deeper connection with Jesus. Constant prayer keeps the lifeline open between God and the believer in their spirit. God is always there and never leaves, so it is that easy to just talk to Him during the drive to work, cleaning the house, taking a shower, or anytime really.

Always be prepared to help others. If one person prepared and stocked up on food and the rest of the neighborhood did not, this doesn't mean you have to hand all the stocks out to everyone. This means there will be times when a brother or sister in Christ needs help. Someone may be in a position to invite them into their home for shelter or feed them as they pass through. Whatever God lays on the heart at the time, do it. Help where help can be given, and don't turn away a true brother or sister in Christ. This doesn't apply to giving a week's supply to the drug-addicted couple down the street or the atheist that attacks every Christian in the neighborhood. Take care of God's children. Most of God's children should heed these warnings and have some form of preparation. That doesn't mean they had resources to prepare fully though. Help them whenever and wherever it's needed.

In these last days, Christianity will become more and more against the law. There may even be a point when there is no access to a Bible. It would be wise to know God's Word so that it can still be used in spiritual warfare, praise, worship, and teaching. This will keep the spirit fed with daily bread so that it doesn't starve either.

Above all, trust the Lord. He knows what He is doing. There has been a plan for thousands of years. He knew what part each of His saints would play before they were even born. God is in control, and His will is the most important priority. Put trust in the Lord, and everything will work out the way it is supposed to. In the end, those that have been redeemed will stand in glory next to the Savior for eternity, and that is worth anything. Praise God!

God may speak to some about physical preparations for the tribulation as well. Some might say there is no need for that because God will provide. They cite that He says not to worry about tomorrow and what one will eat or wear. Yes, that is in the Bible, but that is generally speaking for a day-to-day basis. Since God doesn't change, He felt the same way in the book of Genesis but still instructed Noah to gather and stockpile food and to take it with them on the ark (Gen. 6:21–22). There wasn't manna from heaven in this situation. Each instance is according to God's specific instructions. This is why His voice must be obeyed.

Even most federal agencies (such as FEMA, the Nation Weather Service, and others) recommend keeping a thirty-day emergency supply for every house. There are several things His watchmen have been calling out for many years now. One of these is keeping a ready supply of nonperishable food and water stockpiled. It is suggested to have at least thirty days but up to several years' worth of food and clean water available. When considering how much water is needed, estimate a minimum of a gallon a day per person.

There could be many reasons this will be needed. A bad storm could knock out power or prevent travel in and out of the city for a period of time. A natural disaster or war could take power down on a large scale and prevent deliveries to grocery stores. Civil unrest could keep people in their homes for safety reasons. Imagine Ferguson, Missouri on steroids in Dallas, Texas, and surrounding areas that lasted for two months. Every street is engaged in riots, looting, and violence nonstop day and night. It would be a good idea to just stay in the house.

The food stored up should be easy to prepare with no power. That will require things like handheld can openers, plastic utensils and dishes, extra hand sanitizer to save water, anything to cook on that doesn't require gas or electricity or even food that doesn't need cooking. Keep an eye on expiration dates. Have a variety of foods that meet nutritional needs.

Make sure the food available provides protein, calcium, vitamin C and D, carbs, and any other special dietary need each family member may need. There are inexpensive options that can be put back a few dollars at a time as often as possible. Some good items are pinto beans, tuna, canned chicken, spam, white rice, emergency foods with long shelf life (especially for the occasion), ramen noodles, dried pasta, canned pasta sauces, canned soups, canned chili, canned or dehydrated fruits and vegetables, and powdered milk. Multivitamins or specific vitamin supplements could also be a good idea.

Food and water stores are the most important thing, but hygiene items will be of high importance as well. Most people overlook a lot of these things when making an emergency supply kit. Since water is a precious commodity, try to select items that will conserve water. For example, mouthwash can allow for tooth care without as much actual brushing. Brushing could be cut to once or twice a day instead of three times. Hand sanitizer and sanitary wet wipes or baby wipes can eliminate some handwashing. Paper or plastic cups, plates, utensils can eliminate a lot of need for dish care. Get creative.

In general, here is a list of some common things that will need to be addressed. Make sure there is a steady supply of toilet paper, paper towels, oral hygiene needs, feminine hygiene needs, trash bags, deodorant, bleach, general use soap, contact or denture needs, backup pair of glasses, dry shampoo (doesn't need rinsing) just in case, pet needs, diapers and wipes if there are babies, and anything to address whatever specific special needs there may be in the household.

There are plenty of other supplies to stock up on as well. Medications should always be considered ahead of time. First-aid supplies are highly important and should consist of pain relievers, antibiotics, burn creams, bandages, gauze, alcohol, peroxide, triple antibiotic ointments, instant ice packs, solar blankets, iodine, medical tape, and other medicines as needed for allergies, heartburn, gas, cough, and cold, etc. Also add those that address any specific needs, such as diabetes testing strips, blood pressure cuff, or other items according to each household's situation.

Always have plenty of batteries, candles, flashlights, a weather radio, a clean five-gallon bucket (can come in handy for many uses), clothespins and rope, extra gas for any generators or vehicles, something to keep kids busy with no power is helpful, and some hand tools, like an ax, hunting knife, shovel, and hammer. If the home has a gun, extra ammo is a good idea.

Always have bags or backpacks packed and ready to go in case of an emergency that might require evacuation. Wildfires, floods, hurricanes, or any number of things could necessitate a quick exit. See the back for references to better lists in each category and what to include in the to-go bags.

Always have contingency plans for different situations, including a way to continue to have worship service. Where will the family meet if they get separated? If there are no utilities, what will be used for heat and cooking sources, bathroom facilities, and the sleeping arrangements that go with these options? Will other families be in the household? Can an alternate energy source be acquired? Can the house be protected from danger? Are there options for shelter and plans to get there for each situation? Is there a bomb shelter, storm shelter, or evacuation plan for floods, fire, earthquakes, volcanoes, hurricanes, or other instances nearby or available? Always have a plan—and a plan B, C, D, and E. If all this seems a little silly, consider that Noah was given instructions to stockpile and prepare. Consider the events that the book of Revelation and Daniel express and what they could mean for believers. Most of all, consider whatever the Lord speaks to each individual. Everyone should seek the Lord's counsel themselves.

CHAPTER 11

What and When Is the Rapture?

THERE HAS BEEN MUCH DISCUSSION and disagreement among the body of Christ as to when the church will leave this earth. When is the rapture? What does scripture say?

It's an awesome thought to think that before the Antichrist is revealed the church will be raptured out and won't have to endure any tribulation. Anyone would love for that to be true if that is God's will. Who wouldn't? The question at hand is, what does the scripture support? Before this discussion starts, it should be noted that there is a blessing just for reading the book of Revelation all the way through by oneself instead of relying on the church or someone else to convey what it says (Rev. 1:3).

First, at this moment, everyone needs to clear their minds. It doesn't matter who supports pretribulation rapture, midtribulation rapture, rapture after the great tribulation, or no rapture at all. It is asked that, before you read any further, you should go now in prayer to the Lord and ask Him to guide you through this by the Holy Spirit. Ask Him to remove all of your knowledge and everything you think you know. This doesn't mean you are wrong. This means when you are finished reading, the goal is to not have a preconceived, prideful conclusion but an answer guided by God's Word and Spirit. So please pray for discernment, an open mind, and guidance with His love and truth.

The way of a fool is right in his own eyes: but he that hearkeneth unto counsel is wise. (Prov. 12:15)

Let no man deceive himself. If any man among you seemeth to be wise in this world, let him become a fool, that he may be wise. (1 Cor. 3:18)

My people are destroyed for lack of knowledge; because you have rejected knowledge, I reject you from being a priest to me. And since you have forgotten the law of your God, I will also forget your children. (Hosea 4:6)

This is where no one wants to end up. The next thing needed to be addressed is why it is important to know when rapture is. The Bible says no one will know the hour and the day. That is absolutely correct and not the purpose here. Also, it should be added if someone puts a date on it, the devil is deceiving them, and they should be told so and we should pray for them. Matthew does, however, reference that Christians should know the season (Matt. 24). They should know it's "at the door," to use the reference in the Bible. Why do they need to know this?

Most importantly, Revelation warns of adding to or taking away from this book of prophecy (Rev. 22:18–19). Any change could result in plagues or removal of their name from the book of life, resulting in loss of salvation. If it is a pretribulation rapture, as some say, with a second chance at salvation, then they would want to prepare messages for those left behind, as you see some questions posed to this on social media.

If it is a midtribulation rapture, then they would need to know what to be prepared for and what steps as Christians they need to take so that their faith and knowledge of the Word is enough to sustain them through hard times as well as know their jobs as the church in these times. They must know what to expect so they are not deceived by demons and/or false doctrine in the church buildings (1 Tim. 4:1) so as not to get caught in the falling away (2 Thess. 2:3) or be found lukewarm and be spit out of the body of Christ (Rev. 3:15–16). If it is after the great tribulation with no rapture, they must prepare for everything above as well as seeing the bowls of wrath carried out on everyone around them that is not a spirit-filled Christian. This might include being strong enough to witness this with people they love.

It would require them to have such a relationship with the Lord that they can hear His every command and obey without question or hesitation regardless of what they believe the results will be—which they should be doing anyway. If there is no rapture, then they would need to deal with the fact that in the old earth passing away, they would too, and this is after all the above. Then they would rise as the dead in Christ.

So there is a different result and higher need of preparation of faith, strength, and knowledge of the Word to sustain them and, most of all, their relationship with Jesus. Again everyone should strive to attain that highest form of a relationship with Him regardless, but why prepare for tragedies that they might not witness? In the same spirit, why believe they don't need to prepare if in fact they will witness it?

Since it would be the first scenario, the first scripture examined is used to support a pretribulation rapture. The scriptures noted are taught in churches and discussed among Christians as evidence supporting this theory. They will be gone through in context and without changing any words or meanings to fit an idea but instead rightly divide the Word of God. They will be commented on in between each as to the meaning of each scripture, not what is taught it means if it is read in a certain way. There will be no certain order to the scriptures, such as chronological order, order prophecy was given in, etc.—to the scriptures.

For this we say unto you by the word of the Lord, that we which are alive and remain unto the coming of the Lord shall not prevent them which are asleep. For the Lord himself shall descend from heaven with a shout, with the voice of an archangel, and with the trump of God: and the dead in Christ shall rise first: Then we which are alive and remain shall be caught up together in the clouds, to meet the Lord in the air: and so shall we ever be with the Lord. (1 Thess. 4:15–17)

Here is what many Christians believe to be evidence of the rapture as before tribulation. Many say this verse is proof that rapture and the Second Coming are two separate events, that this verse is proof rapture is supposed to be secret and that the Second Coming would be in Revelation and Matthew (Rev. 14:14–16; Matt. 24:29–30). The reason used is that, in this verse, Jesus doesn't come all the way to earth but instead calls the saints upward to the clouds, but when in Revelation, it is noticed that Jesus stays in the clouds in those verses as well.

As a detective would, this verse is broken down into data. It says those that are alive do not prevent those that are asleep but that an angel will appear and sound a trumpet. Then the dead in Christ shall rise first, followed by those that are alive, and all will together rise to Jesus in the clouds to be with Him forever.

Here is the list of all investigative elements here:

- Who: the dead in Christ and those that are still alive that remain
- When: until the coming of the Lord
- What: a gathering in the clouds announced by an angel and a trumpet
- Where: from earth to the clouds.

The time frame in these verses says "until the coming of the Lord." They do not say until the start of tribulation. There is no mention in these verses stating there are two separate events, being the rapture and the Second Coming. As a matter of fact, it clearly says the rapture or being caught up happens to those that remain alive unto the coming of the Lord. There is also no evidence of this being a secret event. It comes with an appearance of an archangel and a sound of a trumpet in the clouds. This doesn't sound secretive or hidden. There are no words in the verses themselves to suggest a secret.

Here is another verse used to speak of the rapture and the Second Coming being separate events.

> Immediately after the tribulation of those days shall the sun be darkened, and the moon shall not give her light, and the stars shall fall from heaven, and the powers of the heavens shall be shaken: And then shall appear the sign of the Son of man in heaven: and then shall all the tribes of earth mourn, and they shall see the Son of man coming in the clouds of heaven with power and great glory. (Matt. 24:29–30)

In these verses, those that support pretribulation rapture would say this is the Second Coming. This verse definitely doesn't say the same thing as 1 Thessalonians (1 Thess. 4:15 –17). After the tribulation of those days, the sun and moon go dark and stars fall from the sky and the powers of the heavens are shaken. Then the sign of the Son of man or Jesus appears in the sky, and everyone mourns and sees Him.

- When: immediately after tribulation of those days
- Where: seeing from earth up to the clouds
- Who: Jesus in heavens and tribes on earth
- What: Second Coming of Jesus

This clearly describes what will happen right before Jesus appears in the clouds but does not say it is a different event. Actually, it infers 1 Thessalonians happens immediately after these verses (1 Thess. 4:15–17). When looking further into Matthew, it is seen that, yes, that is the case. Matthew then says that the elect are gathered, and it shows more detail following (Matt. 24:31; Matt. 24:40–42):

> For God hath not appointed us to wrath, but to obtain salvation by our Lord Jesus Christ. (1 Thess. 5:9)

> For they themselves shew of us what manner of entering in we had unto you, and how ye turned to God from idols to serve the living and true God; And wait for his Son from heaven, whom he raised from the dead, even Jesus, which delivered us from the wrath to come. (1 Thess. 1:9–10)

> Because thou hast kept the word of my patience, I will also keep thee from the hour of temptation, which shall come upon all the world, to try them that dwell upon the earth. (Rev. 3:10)

God has not appointed the saints to wrath. It does not say God has not appointed them to tribulation. The wrath it speaks of here is the wrath of hell or the lake of fire for those in condemnation and not redeemed by Christ. That's what the salvation of Jesus is about. Scripture doesn't support the tribulation being defined as God's wrath. Actually, Revelation refers to this as the devil's wrath (Rev. 12:12). The great tribulation and persecution of the saints is actually the wrath of the Antichrist, not God. It's when the devil himself walks the earth. Neither of these verses state that the saints will be caught up before the tribulation.

The body of Christ will not experience what the sinners do during tribulation because they obtained salvation by the blood of the Lamb, Jesus Christ, which is the same prophetic repeat of the Lamb's blood on the doorposts in Egypt. The blood of Jesus covering over Christians shows the destruction to pass over saints just like in Egypt in the days of Moses. This is also why the plagues of Egypt are being seen around the earth now.

Revelation says that because the saints have kept God's Word, they will be kept from the hour of temptation (Rev. 3:10). That doesn't say *tribulation*. It says *temptation*. If the church keeps putting the word *tribulation* in the place of all these words, then they are changing God's Word to say what they want it to say. They use replacement theology as an excuse, and that is in error. The church and Israel will both see the same things. The church doesn't replace

Israel. That is not good. You don't replace what God said with other meanings so that it meets a common theory.

> Seventy Weeks are determined upon thy people and upon the holy city, to finish the transgression, and to make an end of sins, and to make reconciliation for iniquity, and to bring in everlasting righteousness, and to seal up the vision and prophecy, and to anoint the most Holy. (Dan. 9:24)

> For then shall be a great tribulation, such as was not seen since the beginning of the world to this time, no, nor shall ever be. And except those days shall be shortened, there should no flesh be saved: but for the elect's sake those days will be shortened. (Matt. 24:21–22)

The second verse are the words of Jesus himself. This doesn't just speak of tribulation but specifically of the great tribulation. It will be so bad that if God doesn't shorten the days, there will be no flesh left. So for that reason, it will be shortened. Now for those that speak of a pretribulation rapture, the word *shortened* is used to prove that it is before tribulation. It also says no flesh would be saved. This means if there were rapture before tribulation, then there would still be no flesh saved because they were removed from the earth. What it does prove is that the saints will be here during tribulation and will need the intervention of Jesus.

Lastly, pretribulation supporters would use the following verses. The Bible must be read in context as a whole, and we must not choose which parts to keep or leave out. Therefore, one cannot pick a few verses and claim them to mean one thing when read *with the whole chapter in context, it means something completely different.*

> And after they had held their peace, James answered, saying, Men and brethren, hearken unto me: Simeon hath declared how God at first did visit the Gentiles, to take out of them a people

for His name. And to this agree the words of the prophets; as it is written, After this I will return, and will build again the tabernacle of David, which is fallen down; and I will build again the ruins thereof, and I will set it up: That the residue of men might seek after the Lord, and all the Gentiles, upon whom my name is called, saith the Lord, who doeth all these things. Known unto God are all his works from the beginning of the world. (Acts 15:13–18)

This would be very convincing—if one does not read the whole chapter in its context. This chapter discusses how Paul, Barnabas, and James were teaching the church that Gentiles do not need to be circumcised to be saved. If they were not already, they do not have to now be circumcised like a Jew to receive the grace of Jesus Christ because Jesus died for all, Jews and Gentiles alike. "Take out of them a people" in this passage means that just like in Revelation 18:4, the Gentiles come out of the nonbelievers into the blood of Jesus Christ and salvation.

Then, after the time allotted for Gentiles and Jews alike to have the chance to be born again, a temple will be rebuilt on the ruins of the old temple. What this passage holds for believers as far as prophecy for the end of days is that the temple will be rebuilt on the same site it was torn down and not somewhere else. This will happen so that people can see that Bible prophecy has come true just as God promised and they might come to the Lord, knowing the Bible is not a lie.

After this I looked, and behold, a door was opened in heaven: and the first voice which I heard was as it were of a trumpet talking with me; which said, Come up hither and I will shew thee things which must be hereafter. (Rev. 4:1)

Behold, I shew you a mystery; we shall not sleep, but we shall all be changed, in a moment, in the

> twinkling of an eye, at the last trump: for the
> trumpet shall sound, and the dead shall be raised
> incorruptible, and we shall be changed. (1 Cor.
> 15:51–52)

This needs to be broken down because this obviously describes the moment of rapture.

- Who: the saints (those alive or the ones that shall not sleep) and the dead
- What: changed in a moment, in the twinkling of an eye
- Where: earth because that is where the dead are
- When: at the last trumpet when it sounds

This verse is the most revealing verse found. It tells exactly when rapture will happen. It occurs at the last trumpet. John states the resurrection will take place on the last day (John 6:40, 44, 54). Taking these in context, this shows rapture will happen on the last day at the last trumpet. The book of Revelation shows what must happen before the rapture.

The next point of discussion is a midtribulation rapture. There are some Christians that support rapture after tribulation but before the great tribulation. This is called a midtribulation rapture. This view supports that the saints will not be here to make the choice of the mark of the beast. In Matthew, it states all saints will be persecuted just like the prophets before them (Matt. 5:11–12). Also Matthew reads that Jesus doesn't come to bring peace but a sword (Matt. 10:34–35). These verses are used by midtribulation supporters to say Christians will be here for tribulation. They say it shows proof of persecution during tribulation and that Jesus has no intention of things being peaceful. That is exactly correct.

The first verse alone could mean persecution at any time throughout history, but when the book of Matthew is taken in context with other chapters and verses, we see that this is meant for the persecution during tribulation during the fifth seal. The midtribulation aspect, however, does not take into account that this also concerns this persecution of the saints and choice of the mark of the beast in the great tribulation. Through the hedge of protection of Jesus, believers escape these trials except for persecution (Psalm 91). Just like in Egypt, when they marked the doorposts with lamb's blood, Christians mark their hearts with the blood of the Lamb by accepting Jesus and surrendering our lives fully to Him.

Those that support midtribulation (or pre–great tribulation) rapture use Matthew 24:1–31 to prove the saints will be here for tribulation even though they are exempt from the wrath of God and that there is no pretribulation rapture. Now along with this scripture, Mark 13:1–27 and Luke 21:1–28 are cited as well. Since these passages are three different accounts of the same speech from Jesus as He was talking to all the apostles at that moment, this one commentary can be applied to those as well, though there are some minor differences as there is more detail in some of the other books.

For example, Mark tells where believers might be delivered to for persecution and not to preplan what to say but to let the Holy Spirit speak instead. He also gives more detail as to who will betray whom. Luke talks about great earthquakes and adds fearful sights in the sign of tribulation as well as who will betray whom.

Luke also says, and this is important, that even though the saints will be here, Christians should not to worry about tribulation because not a hair on their head will be harmed. Luke adds that with the abomination of desolation, Israel will also be encompassed with armies and people will fall by the sword and be taken captive, and he adds that the sea and waves will be roaring, men's hearts failing them in fear, and distress of nations to the signs in the heavens and the signs right before the return of Jesus.

In Matthew, it can be seen that Jesus is speaking of the great tribulation (Matt. 24). First, He calls it the great tribulation by name, and secondly, it is after the abomination that causes desolation, which is the start of the great tribulation. He describes rapture and the elect being gathered after the events in the great tribulation. Jesus shows the order of events clearly. A midtribulation rapture theory calls Jesus a liar. This passage does, as the midtribulation (pre–great tribulation) supporters say, prove the saints will be here for tribulation. It also proves that they will be here for the great tribulation.

This would move discussion on to a midtribulation rapture or, as some would call it, posttribulation/prewrath rapture, depending on whether they have studied the scripture for a difference between the great tribulation and the wrath of God.

There are two different words for *wrath* in the Greek form in which the New Testament was originally written. One is essentially translated to "outburst of anger or wrath," and the other is "settled wrath," both of which in the English translation just say *wrath*. Now the "outburst of anger" is used nine times in Revelation, and "settled wrath" is used twenty-seven times throughout the New Testament, all of which never subjects a believer to the wrath (Rom. 1:18; John 3:36). The word *tribulation* is used fifty-five times, and forty-seven of those experiences are endured by believers. This would definitely show a difference in the biblical definitions of *wrath* and *tribulation* (Lemke, "Biblical Case for Mid-Tribulationism"). The tribulation and the great tribulation according to scripture is not the same thing. They are two separate events, and God's wrath is another event entirely.

So now there is one option left to discuss. It is posttribulation rapture because the great tribulation and the wrath of God are in fact two different things according to scripture. This next discussion is fully supported by scripture. Everyone, of course, must seek the Holy Spirit themselves. This will actually walk through the whole book of Revelation though chapter 14. If anyone would like to grab their Bible and follow along, they can see the context in between.

First, here are a few other points. The church and Israel are not separate, and everything will happen for them together. Israel and the saints are one people—together, the children of God according to Romans and John (Rom. 11, 2:28–29, 9:6–8; John 17:21). Israel, according to the Bible, is all the Gentiles and all the Jews that have accepted Jesus into their hearts. That is what the Bible considers the children of God. Everyone else is considered the children of the devil. Israel and the church are one and will always remain so. So there cannot be a tribulation for Israel and not for the church. There is a tribulation for all of God's children.

Christians will be here for tribulation. The rapture does not come before tribulation. It doesn't come before the great tribulation after the last trumpet, as pointed out already in 1 Corinthians and Matthew (1 Cor. 15:51–52; Matt. 24:29–30). As a matter of fact, even the resurrection comes before the rapture according to 1 Thessalonians (1 Thess. 4:16–17). Christians will be here to see the Antichrist and all his evil deeds. There are things that must happen before rapture can occur. The Bible doesn't lie, and people can't use that replacement theology bologna trying to make it say what they want it to because they are afraid. What are they afraid of? They died already. On the day a person gave their life to Christ, they died, and it is now Christ who lives in them.

Fear nothing but the Lord. The Antichrist is already defeated. Read the back of the book. The saints will see the Antichrist. Let no man deceive anyone. So when the world kicks God out of their countries, their churches by teaching false doctrine, their homes by not living like He told us and following the lusts of the flesh, and their lives, then He is no longer there and will not prevent the Antichrist from coming.

The coming of Jesus and the gathering to Him cannot happen until after the falling away and the Antichrist is revealed. It can't happen until after the Antichrist completes the abomination that causes desolation and the false prophet shows false miracles and signs (2 Thess. 2:1–10). When the Antichrist is revealed, everyone that didn't already receive the love of the truth will be deceived and not be saved. God will make them believe the lie so that all who did not believe the truth but had pleasure in unrighteousness will be damned.

Those are strong words. No one else can come to salvation after the Antichrist is revealed. (2 Thess. 2:1–10). That is at the start of tribulation. That means the saints in tribulation are the ones already saved and born again when tribulation starts. That means there is no rapture of the saints right before tribulation starts, or there would be no saints in tribulation. Still confused? Try this one.

> And all that dwell upon the earth shall worship
> him, whose names are not written in the book of

life of the Lamb slain from the foundation of the world. (Rev. 13:8)

If a Christian is found lukewarm, then they are spued or vomited out of the body of Christ and no longer in the book of life (Rev. 3:15–16). Know this, if a person is not truly saved—not a fake Christian, but "walking the walk" saved—then when the Antichrist is revealed, they *will* worship him and take the mark of the beast and can't say they won't because God said he is going to make them. God can do whatever He wants.

There are only two entities in this world that truly know the status of a person's salvation—Jesus and that person. If they aren't walking the walk, then Jesus isn't in their heart. They may believe in Him, but they don't know or truly love Him if they are walking constantly in the lust of the flesh. Now that doesn't mean an occasional slipup. Salvation isn't a free ticket to sin. Here goes the book of Revelation play by play.

Revelation says this is a vision given to John (Rev. 1:1). It shows a future tense vision of Jesus coming in the clouds (Rev. 1:7). Those that pierced Jesus can only see Him if the resurrection that happens right before rapture happens with the Second Coming of Christ and not before tribulation in secret. It says Jesus will keep the saints from the hour of temptation to test those on earth (Rev. 3:10). It doesn't say the hour of tribulation. It says He will keep them from the temptation. This speaks of the temptation to deny Christ and take the mark of the beast in order to escape death. The saints will be given strength, not removed from earth.

Revelation tells lukewarm Christians that do not follow God's commandments and sin purposely that they will be removed or vomited out of the body of Christ (Rev. 3:15 –16). Their salvation will be lost. The Antichrist arrives here on earth (Rev. 6:2). It doesn't say for sure whether or not he is revealed yet. Since John was still speaking to the churches in chapter 3 and in 5:8 the beasts and elders had vials of saints prayers, it is known that, at this point, the saints are still on earth. Peace is taken from the earth with the red horseman and the second seal broken (Rev. 6:4).

The third seal is broken, and the black horse, which is economic despair and famine, arrives. The fourth seal, the pale horse—death with the power to kill one-fourth of the earth by the sword with hunger, death, and by the beasts of the earth—comes next (Rev. 6:7 –8). Then there is the fifth seal in Revelation (Rev. 6:9–11). The saints that weren't killed are still here. The rapture hasn't happened yet. This even says those saints are still resting. They're not in heaven; they are still in the ground.

Then there is the sixth seal, which happens on the last day, the day of the Lord, the day of wrath (Rev. 6:12–17). Revelation says not to harm anything until the seals of God have been placed (Rev. 7:3). That means the saints are still here. Revelation 9:4 orders that those with the seal of God will not be harmed by the locusts. That shows the saints are still here. The trumpets continue to sound, and it proceeds to Revelation 10, where six trumpets have sounded. The saints still haven't gone anywhere.

The temple is rebuilt and Jerusalem is split and the two witnesses come and go (Rev. 11). The serpent makes war with the saints (Rev. 12). This is concurrent with Revelation 13, in which the saints are still on earth and have not been raptured yet. The beast system rises along with the one world government and the Antichrist. It is at war with the saints that are still on earth (Rev. 13:7). These same saints that were here when tribulation started are the saints that must choose the mark of the beast or beheading. Revelation continues, and the saints are still here until chapter 14:14–16.

This is the moment of the resurrection and rapture. There is no more mention of the saints on earth after this point until the new heaven and new earth in Revelation 21. The rapture and resurrection happen on the last day of the great tribulation, followed by a quick issuance of the treading of the winepress and an almost simultaneous seven bowls of wrath.

The next day is the millennial kingdom. Revelation 18:8 states these all happen in one day. As can be seen, there is no other option but a resurrection and then rapture after tribulation but before the bowls of wrath. Scripture just doesn't support it. If anyone is deceived, they could fall away. Their faith and spirit won't be prepared because they will still be in shock, expecting to have been gone.

Please do not be deceived. Everyone should study these scriptures and not rely on pastors and Bible colleges to teach them something that hasn't always been taught. The pretribulation rapture theory came about with John Darby and the Calvinistic movement in AD 1830. It has only been taught for less than two hundred years, and there is a reason for that. This was not taught by the apostles or any other church that can be found before John Darby. This is a lie from the devil meant to deceive people into falling away. This leads to another question. If the saints are still here, why are they still here?

CHAPTER 12

Why Is the Body of Christ Still Here?

SO CONSIDER TRIBULATION HAS STARTED, or even the great tribulation has started, and there was no rapture. The saints are still here. There will be many that believed the false doctrine of a pretribulation rapture and cannot understand why they are still here or will swear that tribulation couldn't have started yet because they are still here. Why are the saints still here? Why would Jesus leave them here to go through this? What do the saints do now? How do the believers endure? There are so many questions. Not all these questions have precise answers. This last chapter will discuss a few concerns and reasons to answer some of the many that are surely spinning in many people's heads.

Why are the saints still here? Never in the whole Bible has God removed anyone from earth to protect them from judgment that was not meant for them. He simply kept them from the situation. Look at the cases of Noah and Lot. Neither men nor their families were taken off earth. In Noah's case, it was the whole earth that was flooded, but they were still left here on earth and given a hedge of protection and instructions to keep them safe. Lot was guided by angels away from the danger to an area where there was no danger. His family was given instructions to keep them safe as well, and all those that followed the instructions were safe. The one that did not and looked back didn't make it.

Jesus tells the saints ahead of time that they will be delivered up to be afflicted, killed, and hated (Matt. 24:9; Matt. 10:22; Mark 13:9–13; Luke 21:12–19). Why would Jesus lie? He doesn't because

He's perfect. The saints aren't supposed to assume that everything will be easy. Christ didn't die so that the saints don't have to experience tribulation. He died so they don't have to experience the true wrath of God, which is the lake of fire or hell. He died so that there is no condemnation for God's children. He died to take away the sins of those that will follow Him, not to give them an exit stage left when times get hard. He came to bring a sword, not peace, on earth (Matt. 10:34–39). He came to set man against his father and daughter against her mother, and that man's foes will be in their own household.

Jesus expects believers to love Him more than anything. If given the choice between their mother, father, children, and Him, they should choose Jesus. There is a reason for that. One day the believers may have to watch those loved ones die unless they deny Jesus. Only by loving Jesus more can the situation be overcome. That's why Jesus said, "He that taketh not his cross and follow after me is not worthy of me and to find their life is to lose it but to lose it is to find it." This means there will be a cross to carry. The cross is not easy. It is a hard, long, horrible road to a bloody death that ended in life eternal. It was gruesome and horrific.

This means it is a burden that is worth it, not an easy road that ends in rainbows and unicorns. He specifically says those that save their life in the flesh will in reality lose their life. Those that lose their life in the flesh will gain it for eternity in heaven. There is a beautiful gift that comes with the horrible persecution (Matt 5:11–12). All this is supported in Matthew, Mark, and Luke as well (Matt. 10:16–25, 16:24–26; Mark 8:34; Luke 9:23). There is a very different question that should be seen here. Why when Jesus has told believers this will happen would they create stories to try to avoid it? Why do some believers think they are better than Jesus? If the world hates Jesus, it hates believers too (John 15:18–21). The servant is not greater than his Lord. Why do believers think they deserve any less than what Jesus received?

Christians are God's soldiers (2 Tim. 3:12). Soldiers die in battle. There are casualties in war. The saints are supposed to rejoice and be happy that they are to partake in Christ's sufferings and reproach and glorify Him because of it (1 Pet. 4:12–19). Instead there are those that would create false doctrine and deceive 90 percent of the church into thinking that the saints won't be here at all even though Jesus specifically warned the church it would happen and might deceive the very elect.

There is no promise it will be easy or that Christians will escape this. There is only reward for enduring it and rest afterward (Rev. 14:12–13). Those that push a notion that they will be kept from what Jesus has appointed to the saints are actually insulting the work done for them on the cross by assuming they are better than Jesus, the apostles, and all believers dying right now in the name of Jesus.

This isn't meant to offend purposely, but it is meant to share undeniable biblical truth, and if biblical truth is offensive, then so be it. These are the last days. This is the last generation. Those in Christ have no reason or cause to be afraid of anything. Rejoice in the fact that eternity is right around the corner. Endure in faith and love.

The saints need to prepare their houses in every way possible. Even Noah prepared for the flood on God's order. This watchman is crying out, sounding the trumpet in these last days, begging everyone to take heed. The enemy is attacking, and tribulation is just around the corner. It isn't conspiracy theory when it comes from Bible prophecy and scripture. Everyone that truly takes up their cross and follows Jesus on the narrow path to eternal life will be persecuted in some form. There will be those that make it to rapture. There will be those that give their life in testimony to Jesus.

Trust in the Lord, and keep the focus on Jesus. When fear creeps in, just praise His holy name until it passes. If the saints follow God's will and instructions, no harm will come to them except for persecution, which is an honor and gains many crowns. Keep the faith, fight the good fight, endure until the end, and we will meet at the final trumpet. God bless everyone, and may Jesus keep all the saints.

How to Be Born Again

JESUS CAN SAVE ANYONE FROM any situation. His love, mercy, grace, and redemption know no bounds. They are limitless, and it doesn't matter what anyone has done. Someone could have sold their soul to the devil, and Jesus could still fix it. He loves every person that ever walked or will walk the face of this earth. That's why He died on the cross for the world while all were still sinners.

There is no other way into heaven, and salvation comes by no other name. One must accept that Jesus Christ is the Son of God sent here to save them, was crucified on the cross, and resurrected on the third day, defeating the grave and death. They must confess and repent of their sins to the Lord—no one else, just God. They must surrender their lives, bodies, minds, souls, hearts, and everything to Jesus. They must admit they are a sinner and ask to be washed in the blood of the Lamb and made clean and be born again.

Time is running out. Please seek the Lord while He may be found before it is too late. No one has to fix anything before they come to Jesus. Let Him fix the broken pieces. Just come just as you are right here and now. If you truly want to change your life, bow your head, and pray this prayer. Tell Jesus you are His.

> Heavenly Father,
>
> I come to you now as a sinner. I know Jesus, Your Son, died on the cross to save me from my sins and was raised from the grave. Jesus, I ask that

you come into my life. Break me, and rebuild me, Lord, and make me new again. Wash me clean in the blood of the Lamb, and make me whole again. Forgive me of my sins, Lord, and help and teach me to walk in light and not in darkness. I repent of all my sins and renounce all other gods and spirits. I take up my cross, Lord, and follow you. Make me born again. Break any curses, demonic strongholds, addictions, and all chains on me, Lord. Heal my body, spirit, and mind. Empty me of me so that I can be filled with You, Jesus. Show me the way, the truth, and the life through You, Jesus, and help me walk the narrow path. Thank you for making me born again, born of the Spirit into life eternal with You.

In Jesus's name, I pray. Amen.

How to Be Baptized in the Holy Spirit

WHEN A PERSON IS BORN again or saved, the Holy Spirit comes to live in their heart. This is not the same as the baptism of the Holy Spirit or infilling of the Holy Spirit. When a person receives the gift of the Holy Ghost, his whole body is enveloped, and the Holy Spirit overflows out of the heart and surrounds the person completely. It is just like when the water surrounds a person during a water baptism and that person is totally engulfed in water.

During the baptism of the Holy Spirit, He overflows out of the heart of a born-again Christian and overtakes the whole body. It is at this time that one receives the gifts of the Spirit, as spoken of in 1 Corinthians 12; included is a prayer language so that they may pray in the Spirit or tongues (Mark 16:17–19). Some can receive the baptism of the Holy Spirit at the moment they are saved, and on many God must do a little work first to help them remove doubt or other things that might keep them from receiving the Holy Ghost.

The Holy Ghost is a gift from God to every born-again believer with no requirement other than being born again. Just like any gift, it must be received and accepted. It can be turned away. Fear of walking in God's power, doubt, pride, and spiritual wounds or strongholds are some of the biggest reasons why it can be blocked, sometimes without even knowing it. One can only receive the Holy Ghost if they are already saved.

If you have not received the baptism of the Holy Spirit since you believed, then follow these steps. It is very important that you do. It is a command from God in Acts 2:38.

126

1. Prepare yourself. Confess all your sins to God. You don't need anyone else to be there. It's between you and the Lord, and that's it. Tell Him if you don't think you can remember everything and just ask Him to help you. He doesn't expect perfection out of anyone but Jesus. Renounce any works of darkness—such as witchcraft, occult, false religions, and New-Age practices, like horoscopes, yoga, holistic healing.

2. The next step can be done alone or with someone already baptized in the Holy Spirit if you feel you want some help. I was alone but was also watching Anita Fuentes from EMOAF.org, and she prayed with us. Simply go to God in prayer, and ask Jesus to baptize you in the Holy Spirit and refine you in the fire. Don't beg or plead with Him, but just ask and have faith, and know it will be done because you asked. Want it, mean it, and believe it.

3. All that you must do now is accept the gift. Receive the gift of the Holy Ghost. The devil will start lying to you, causing doubts. He will tell you that you don't need to do this and speaking in tongues isn't important or isn't of God. Ignore the devil, and don't give him place. Keep your focus on Jesus, and praise His holy name until the doubt passes. Thank Jesus out loud for the gift of the Holy Ghost with the evidence of other tongues.

4. Next just release your holy language. You must move your mouth and tongue. You must make your voice work, but God will give you the words or utterance. Trust that when you start to talk, it will be God giving you a heavenly language. Don't think about how it sounds, but instead, just let it flow.

There are several helpful articles in the "For More Information Section" that can be very helpful. Also www.emoaf.org or www. openyoureyespeople.com has several videos available. This web address is one of them. It's titled "Pentecost Sunday June 8th 2014 and the Baptism of the Holy Spirit" (https://www.youtube.com/watch?v=flLSOHvzmUo&app=desktop).

Bibliography

"Asia Pacific Food Situation Update–July 2010–Myanmar…" ReliefWeb. July 31, 2010. Accessed May 22, 2016. *http://reliefweb. int/report/myanmar/asia-pacific-food-situation-update-july-2010.*

Associated Press. "Chinese Christians Fight Back as Government Tears down…" FoxNews.com. July 25, 2014. Accessed May 3, 2016. http://www.foxnews.com/world/2014/07/25/as-government-tears-down-church-crosses-chinese-christians-rise-to-defend-their.html.

Associated Press. "Somalia: Famine Toll in 2011 Was Larger Than Previously…" NYTimes.com. April 29, 2013. Accessed May 3, 2016. http://www.nytimes.com/2013/04/30/world/africa/somalia-famine-toll-in-2011-was-larger-than-previously-reported.html.

Associated Press. "Iraq Drought Its Marshes in Garden of Eden." NBCNews.com. April 29, 2013. Accessed May 21, 2016. *http:// www.nbcnews.com/id/30227029/ns/weather/t/iraq-drought-hits-marshes-garden-eden/#.WAwpco-cGUk.*

Associated Press. "Termites Strike Central Fla. School District– Story…" ABCActionNew.com. March 11, 2013. Accessed May 22, 2016. http://www.abcactionnews.com/news/state/termites-strike-central-florida-school-district.

Avila, Jim. "Jesus of Suburbia-Has He Risen Again in Houston, Texas?" ABCNews.go.com. March 6, 2007. Accessed May 3, 2016. http://abcnews.go.com/Primetime/story?id=2925021&page=1.

Bakalar, Nicholas. "Plague Cases in the U.S. on the Rise." Well Blogs NYTimes.com, September 7, 2015. Accessed May 22, 2016. http://well.blogs.nytimes.com/2015/09/07/plague-cases-in-u-s-on-the-rise/.

Bautz, Friedrich W., and Traugott Bautz. Biographisch-bibliographisches Kirchenlexikon: Bd. 23. 2843 Nordhausen: Bautz, 2004. Print. As translated and cited in Wikipedia.

"BBC NEWS | Europe | French Heat Toll Almost 15,000." BBC News. September 25, 2003. Accessed May 22, 2016. http://news.bbc.co.uk/2/hi/europe/3139694.stm.

Bowcott, Owen, and Sam Jones. "Isis Persecution of Iraqi Christians Has Become Genocide..." TheGuardian.com. August 9, 2014. Accessed May 22, 2016. https://www.theguardian.com/world/2014/aug/08/isis-persecution-iraqi-christians-genocide-asylum.

News Release. "Bubonic Plague Diagnosed in Yellowstone Visitor | SVI News." SVI. August 25, 2008. Accessed May 22, 2016. https://www.starvalleyindependent.com/2008/08/25/bubonic-plague-diagnosed-in-yellowstone-visitor/.

Buchele, Mose. "US Geological Survey to Increase Earthquake Risk Levels in..." StateImpact.NPR.org. January 15, 2015. Accessed May 22, 2016. https://stateimpact.npr.org/texas/2015/01/21/us-geological-survey-to-increase-earthquakes-risk-levels-in-texas/.

Budde, M.E., D.J. Rowland, and P.J. Verdin. "Assessing Impacts of the 2008 Drought on Winter Wheat..." Ipdaa.USGS.gov. November 2008. Accessed May 22, 2016. https://lpdaac.usgs.gov/sites/default/files/public/user_community/docs/Assessing_Impacts_of_the_2008_Drought.pdf.

Bugliosi, Vincent, and Curt Gentry. Helter Skelter: The True Story of the Manson Murders. 25th ed. New York, NY: Norton, 1994.

Burke, Daniel. "Millennials Leaving Church in Droves, Study Says– CNN.com." CNN.com. May 14, 2015. Accessed May 22, 2016. *http://www.cnn.com/2015/05/12/living/pew-religion-study/index.html.*

Cahn, Jonathan. The Harbinger. Lake Mary, FL: FrontLine, 2011.

Cahn, Jonathan. The Mystery of the Shemitah. Lake Mary, FL: FrontLine, 2014.

Canadian Press. "Pine Beetle Finds New Home: Alta. Researchers– Edmonton…" CBC.ca. November 20, 2011. Accessed May 21, 2016. http://www.cbc.ca/news/canada/edmonton/pine-beetle-finds-new-home-alta-researchers-1.1094167.

Canadian Press. "Pine Beetles Defying Anti-Infestation Efforts in Alberta…" CTVNews.ca. November 20, 2011. Accessed May 21, 2016. *http://www.ctvnews.ca/pine-beetles-defying-anti-infestation-efforts-in-alberta-1.728672.*

Carroll, Linda. "Worldwide Surge in 'Great' Earthquakes Seen in Past 10…" NBCNews.com. October 25, 2014. Accessed May 22, 2016. http://www.nbcnews.com/science/science-news/worldwide-surge-great-earthquakes-seen-past-10-years-n233661.

CBC News. "Pine Beetles Continue to Infest Alberta Trees– Edmonton…" CBC.ca. July 14, 2009. Accessed May 21, 2016. *http://www.cbc.ca/news/canada/edmonton/pine-beetles-continue-to-infest-alberta-trees-1.826495.*

Chance, Matthew. "Locust Swarms Plague Southern Russia." CNN.com. August 5, 2015. Accessed May 3, 2016. *http://www.cnn.com/2015/08/04/europe/russia-locust-swarms/index.html.*

CIA. CIA.gov. Accessed May 21, 2016. *https://www.cia.gov/library/publications/the-world-factbook/geos/pa.html.*

Clark, Heather. "Military Chaplains Sue After Being Ordered Not to Quote…" ChristianNews.net. November 10, 2003. Accessed May 4, 2016. *http://christiannews.net/2013/11/10/military-chaplains-sue-after-being-ordered-not-to-quote-bible-pray-in-jesus-name/.*

Conners, Deanna. "Are Large Earthquakes Increasing in Frequency? | Earth..." EarthSky.org. March 4, 2012. Accessed May 1, 2016. *http://earthsky.org/earth/are-large-earthquakes-increasing-in-frequency*.

Conrad, Glenn R. Louisiana Historical Association/Publications/ Dictionary of Louisiana Biography/ Dictionary L/Leon, Count. 1988. Accessed May 26, 2016. *http://lahistory.org/site29.php*.

"Countries Affected by Global Food Crisis Receive Extra..." ReliefWeb. August 8, 2008. Accessed May 21, 2016. *http://relief-web.int/report/burkina-faso/countries-affected-global-food-crisis-receive-extra-funding-un-central-emergency*.

Craig, Mary. "Complete the Mandate." Mary Craig Ministries. November 2002. Accessed May 21, 2016. *http://marycraigministries.com/NewsViews/CompleteTheMandate.htm*.

Crowd Packs Amphitheater for Man Claiming He's Jesus Christ Reincarnated." News6 WKMG ClickOrlando.com. May 8, 2007. Accessed July 5, 2007. www.clickorlando.com. Archived from the original. No longer available.

Crowell, George T. "North Korea in 1996." Encyclopaedia Britannica Online. December 29, 1996. Accessed May 22, 2016. https://www.britannica.com/place/North-Korea-Year-In-Review-1996.

Crugnale, James. "Locusts Threaten to Devastate Argentinian Agriculture." The Weather Channel. January 28, 2016. Accessed May 22, 2016. https://weather.com/science/environment/news/locusts-invade-argentina.

Curry, David. "North Korean Reality Isn't Funny for Christians: Column." USAToday.com. December 25, 2014. Accessed May 4, 2016. http://www.usatoday.com/story/opinion/2014/12/25/interview-north-korea-kim-jong-un-christians-religion-column/20831361/.

"Devastating Wildfire Evacuates All of Fort McMurray..." The Weather Channel. May 13, 2016. Accessed May 13, 2016. *https://weather.com/slideshows/news/fort-mcmurray-wildfire-images*.

Edwards, Steven. "'You Are a Target': Muslim Extremists Terrorize Egypt's…" FoxNews.com. May 5, 2015. Accessed May 22, 2016. http://www.foxnews.com/world/2015/05/05/outside-cairo-egypt-christians-face-persecution.html.

Entomological Society of America. "Study examines bed bug infestations in 2,372 low-income apartments in New Jersey." ScienceDaily. www.sciencedaily.com/releases/2016/04/160405105551.htm (accessed May 27, 2016).

Fleshler, David. "Invasive Lionfish Infestation Discovered by South Florida…" The Huffington Post. June 28, 2013. Accessed May 22, 2016. *http://www.huffingtonpost.com/2013/06/29/lionfish-florida_n_3519596.html.*

Foley, James A. "Biblical Locust Plague Threatens Madagascar: News…" NatureWorldNews.com. March 26, 2013. Accessed May 22, 2016. *http://www.natureworldnews.com/articles/1027/20130326/biblical-locust-plague-threatens-madagascar.htm.*

Fuentes, Anita. "Live On-line Bible Class Course Sessions–EMOAF Church/ EMOAF Biblical Session 2, Course 12, Spiritual Warfare and the Believer's Authority 'Being Led by the Holy Spirit to Wage War'." Evangelistic Ministry of Anita Fuentes. March 31, 2016. Accessed April 7, 2016. *http://www.emoaf.org/Live-online-bible-study-sessions.html.*

Gallart, Oriol Andres. "Drought and Misuse Behind Lebanon's Water Scarcity | Inter…" Inter Press Service. July 28, 2014. Accessed May 22, 2016. http://www.ipsnews.net/2014/07/drought-and-misuse-behind-lebanons-water-scarcity/.

Gedan, Benjamin N. "Uruguay Drought Creates Energy Crisis–Latin American Studies." Latin American Studies. May 25, 2008. Accessed October 25, 2016. *http://latinamericanstudies.org/uruguay/drought.htm.*

Gledhill, Ruth. "Christian Missionary Sentenced to 10 Years Labor North Korea." Christian Today. May 2, 2016. Accessed May 3,

2016. *http://www.christiantoday.com/article/christian.missionary. sentenced.to.10.years.hard.labour.in.north.korea/85194.htm.*

Gráda, Cormac Ó. Famine: A Short History. Princeton, NJ: Princeton University Press, 2009

"Hebrew Roots/Neglected Commandments/Idolatry/Easter..." WikiBooks. March 29, 2016. Accessed May 31, 2016. *https:// en.wikibooks.org/wiki/Hebrew_Roots/Neglected_Commandments/ Idolatry/Easter.*

Hill, Cole. "'Severe' Locust Plague Attacks Madagascar, Needs More Than..." Latinos Post. March 28, 2013. Accessed May 27, 2016. *http://www.latinospost.com/articles/15480/20130328/ severe-locust-plague-attacks-madagascar-needs-more-22m-fight- swarm.htm.*

The Holy Bible, King James Version. Nashville, TN: Holman Bible, 1998.

Human Security Report Project at the School for International Studies, Simon Fraser University. "The Death Toll in the Democratic Republic of the Congo." In Human Security Report 2009/2010: The Cause for Peace and the Shrinking Costs of War, Chapter 3. 43rd ed. Oxford U., 2011. 2011. Accessed May 31, 2016. http://hsrgroup.org/docs/ Publications/HSR2009/2009HumanSecurityReport_Pt2_3_ DeathTollDemocraticRepublicCongo.pdf.

J., B. S. "Drought in Cochabamba- Angostura Photographs." Bolivia Today (blog), November 4, 2007. Accessed May 21, 2016. *http://www.sharingbolivia.com/2007/11/draught-in-cochabam- ba-angostura.html.*

Jensen, Tina. "NWS Radar Picks up ABQ Grasshopper Infestation | KRQE News 13." KRQE News 13. May 30, 2014. Accessed May 27, 2016. *http://krqe.com/2014/05/30/ nws-radar-picks-up-abq-grasshopper-infestation/.*

Jerusalem Post Editorial "Drought & the Treasury–Opinion– Jerusalem Post." *The Jerusalem Post.* January 21, 2009. Accessed

May 22, 2016. *http://www.jpost.com/Opinion/Editorials/ Drought-and-the-Treasury.*

Jie-Ae, Sohn. "CNN–North Korea Receives Aid to Avert Famine– June 11, 1996." CNN Archives. June 11, 1996. Accessed May 27, 2016. http://www.cnn.com/WORLD/9606/11/south. korea/.

Johnson, M. A., Staff Writer. "'Killer Bees' Leave Texas Man Dead, Woman in Serious…" NBCNews.com. June 2, 2013. Accessed May 22, 2016. *http://usnews.nbcnews.com/_ news/2013/06/02/18703314-killer-bees-leave-texas-man-dead-woman-in-serious-condition.*

"Killer Bees Swarming into Oklahoma–News9.com." News9.com. April 26, 2012. Accessed May 22, 2016. *http://www.news9.com/ story/17797976/killer-bees-swarming-into-oklahoma.*

Klaus, Krista. "Flea Infestation Invades Tampa Bay Area | TBO.com." Tampa Bay Times TBO.com. November 6, 2007. Accessed May 21, 2016. *http://www.tbo.com/news/ flea-infestation-invades-tampa-bay-area-165569.*

Lankov, Andrei. "N Korea and the Myth of Starvation–Al Jazeera English." Al Jazeera. March 27, 2014. Accessed May 27, 2016. *http://www.aljazeera.com/indepth/opinion/2014/03/n-korea-myth-starvation-2014319124439924471.html.*

Lee, Jolie. "Grasshopper Outbreak Surfaces on Weather Radar–USA TODAY." USA Today. June 3, 2014. Accessed May 22, 2016. *http://www.usatoday.com/story/news/nation-now/2014/06/03/ grasshoppers-new-mexico-weather-service/9906329/.*

Lemke, Steve W. "THE BIBLICAL CASE FOR MID-TRIBULATIONALISM." New Orleans Baptist Theological Seminary. Accessed May 3, 2016. *http://nobts.edu/Faculty/ItoR/ LemkeSW/Personal/midtribulationism.html.*

Lin, Rong-Gong, II. "Quakes Are Increasing, but Scientists Aren't Sure What It…" *Los Angeles Times.* June 2, 2014. Accessed May 22, 2016. *http://www.latimes.com/local/la-me-la-quakes-20140603-story.html.*

Liston, Barbara. "Florida Battles Slimy Invasion by Giant Snails | Reuters." Reuters. April 14, 2013. Accessed May 22, 2016. http://www.reuters.com/article/us-usa-florida-snails-idUSBRE93D05620130414.

Louisiana Historical Association/Publications/Dictionary of Louisiana Biography/ Dictionary L/Leon, Count. 1988. Accessed May 26, 2016. *http://lahistory.org/site29.php.*

McDougall, Heather. "The Pagan Roots of Easter." TheGuardian.com. April 3, 2010. Accessed May 31, 2016. *https://www.theguardian.com/commentisfree/belief/2010/apr/03/easter-pagan-symbolism.*

"Madagascar Hit by 'severe' Plague of Locusts–BBC News." BBC News. March 27, 2013. Accessed May 27, 2016. *http://www.bbc.com/news/world-africa-21955740.*

Malisow, Craig. "Jesus Christ Celebrates His Birthday Yesterday On…" Houston Press. April 23, 2009. Accessed May 27, 2016. *http://www.houstonpress.com/news/jesus-christ-celebrates-his-birthday-yesterday-on-bissonnet-6715615.*

"Man Claims to Be Jesus on 'This Morning'." YouTube. OhYeahRememberThat. Standard YouTube License. July 15, 2013. Accessed May 26, 2016. *https://www.youtube.com/watch?v=P1XaNU20II8.*

Martinez, Rodrigo. "Chile Government Hands out Water in Major Drought | Reuters." Reuters. February 21, 2008. Accessed May 21, 2016. *http://www.reuters.com/article/environment-chile-drought-dc-idUSHO16425520080221.*

Maxfield, Jen. "Bed Bug Infestation in Two Jersey City Apartments." Eyewitness News ABC7. May 9, 2011. Accessed May 22, 2016. *http://abc7ny.com/archive/8120913/.*

Mazza, Ed. "Killer Bee Attack Leaves 1 Dead, 4 Injured in Arizona…" The Huffington Post. October 9, 2014. Accessed May 22, 2016. *http://www.huffingtonpost.com/2014/10/09/killer-bee-attack-arizona_n_5956544.html.*

Moftah, Lora. "Spring Equinox 2015: 3 Things to Know About the Pagan..." International Business Times. March 30, 2015. Accessed May 31, 2016. *http://www.ibtimes.com/spring-equinox-2015-3-things-know-about-pagan-ostara-festival-1853196.*

Mohney, Gillian. "Nevada Burning Man Festival Bugging Out Over...–ABC News." ABCNews.com. August 21, 2015. Accessed May 22, 2016. *http://abcnews.go.com/Health/nevada-burning-man-festival-bugging-insect-swarms/story?id=33227448*

Molstad, Elyse. "Shark Infestation–WJHG." News Channel 7 WJHG.com. March 27, 2013. Accessed May 27, 2016. *http://www.wjhg.com/home/headlines/8120937.html.*

Murray, David. "Jesus and Mary Cult Followers Buy up Land around Kingaroy..." The Courier Mail. March 27, 2011. Accessed May 21, 2016. http://www.couriermail.com.au/news/queensland/jesus-and-mary-cult-followers-buy-up-land-around-kingaroy/story-e6freoof-1226055912664.

"Miami-based 'Antichrist' Banned from Guatemala." DallasNews.com. April 22, 2007. Accessed May 26, 2016. https://web.archive.org/web/20071023184113/http://www.dallasnews.com/sharedcontent/dws/news/world/stories/042207dnrelantichrist.343573a0.html. Archived from the original.

"Mother Tattoos Religious Sect Symbol on Her 3-Year-Old Son..." The Huffington Post. January 31, 2013. Accessed May 22, 2016. http://www.huffingtonpost.com/2013/01/31/mother-tattoo-son_n_2591132.html.

"New York City–Bedbugs! 15 Worst Cities–Pictures..." CBSNews.com. August 25, 2010. Accessed May 22, 2016. *http://www.cbsnews.com/pictures/bedbugs-15-worst-cities/16/.*

Onyanga-Omara, Jane. "Reports: Iran Fires Missile Marked with 'Israel Should Be...'" USA Today. March 9, 2016. Accessed May 27, 2016. *http://www.usatoday.com/story/news/world/2016/03/09/reports-iran-fires-missiles-marked-israel-must-wiped-out/81517488/.*

Oskin, Becky. "Big Earthquakes Double in 2014, But They're Not Linked." Live Science. June 27, 2014. Accessed May 3, 2016. *http://www.livescience.com/46576-more-earthquakes-still-random-process.html.*

"Overwhelmed by Python Infestation, Florida Embraces Cagey..." Yahoo News. October 11, 2013. Accessed May 22, 2016. https://www.yahoo.com/news/overwhelmed-python-infestation-florida-embraces-cagey-solution-145500166.html?ref=gs. From TakePart.com

"The Persecution of Egypt's Coptic Christians–CBS News." CBSNews. com. December 13, 2013. Accessed October 25, 2016. *http://www.cbsnews.com/news/persecution-of-egypts-coptic-christians/.*

Phillips, Tom. "Christians Form Human Shield around Church in 'China's...'" The Telegraph. April 4, 2014. Accessed May 3, 2016. *http://www.telegraph.co.uk/news/worldnews/asia/china/10745248/Christians-form-human-shield-around-church-in-Chinas-Jerusalem-after-demolition-threat*

Pitts, William L., Handbook of Texas Online. "DAVIDIANS AND BRANCH DAVIDIANS | The Handbook of Texas..." Texas State Historical Association. June 12, 2010. Accessed May 26, 2016. *https://tshaonline.org/handbook/online/articles/ird01.*

Potter, Arnold. "Revelations of Potter Christ, the Messenger of the New..." Archive.org. May 19, 2011. Accessed May 26, 2016. *https://archive.org/details/revelationsofpot00pott.*

Price, Laura. "Argentine Drought May Be the Worst in Over 70 Years." Bloomberg.com Bloomberg. January 6, 2012. Accessed May 26, 2016. No longer available.

Reevell, Patrick. "Plagues of Locusts Darken Skies, Threaten Crops in..." ABCNews. July 30, 2015. Accessed May 27, 2016. *http://abcnews.go.com/International/plagues-locusts-darken-skies-threaten-crops-southern-russia/story?id=32778681.*

Reuters. "Locusts Swarm Israel From Egypt Ahead of Passover..." The World Post. March 6, 2015. Accessed October 25, 2016.

http://www.huffingtonpost.com/2013/03/06/locusts-swarm-israel-from-egypt-ahead-of-passover_n_2817103.html.

Rich, Russell R. Those Who Would Be Leaders: (offshoots of Mormonism). 2nd ed. Provo, UT: Extension Publications, Division of Continuing Education, Brigham Young University, 1967.

Rosenbaum, Matthew. "Plague of Locusts Hits California Town–ABC News." ABC News. June 13, 2012. Accessed May 21, 2016. *http://abcnews.go.com/blogs/headlines/2012/06/plague-of-locusts-hits-california-town/.*

Rosner, Hillary. "Pine Beetle Epidemic–National Geographic Magazine." National Geographic. April 2015. Accessed May 22, 2016. *http://ngm.nationalgeographic.com/2015/04/pine-beetles/rosner-text.*

Rubin, Barry. "NY Times: Obama Jump-Started Arab Spring | Clarion Project." The Clarion Project. March 18, 2013. Accessed May 22, 2016. *http://www.clarionproject.org/analysis/nytimes-obama-jump-started-arab*

Santos, Fernando. "Lured by Early Warm Weather, Scorpions Emerge Swarm Arizona Homes." NYTimes.com. April 28, 2016. Accessed May 22, 2016. *http://www.nytimes.com/2016/04/29/us/lured-by-early-warm-weather-scorpions-emerge-to-swarm-arizona-homes.html?_r=0.*

Sharpe, Levi. "A Bug Swarm So Big It Shows Up On…–Popular Science." Popular Science. July 22, 2015. Accessed May 22, 2016. *http://www.popsci.com/huge-swarm-insects-cover-county-texas.*

Shwayder, Maya. "Locusts in Madagascar: UN Needs $41 Million To End the Plague." International Business Times. March 26, 2013. Accessed May 27, 2016. *http://www.ibtimes.com/locusts-madagascar-un-needs-41-million-end-plague-1153269.*

Siegel, Matt. "The Messiah Complex–The Sydney Morning Herald." The Sydney Morning Herald. May 1, 2013. Accessed May 26, 2016. http://www.smh.com.au/national/the-messiah-complex-20130421-2i946.html.

Siegel-Itzkovich, Judy. "NASA Finds: Mediterranean Drought 'worst in 900 Years…" The Jerusalem Post. March 2, 2016. Accessed May 21, 2016. *http://www.jpost.com/Business-and-Innovation/ Environment/NASA-studies-tree-rings-and-finds-Mediterranean-drought-worst-in-900-years-446653.*

Siff, Andrew. "Gettin' Buggy With It: New Yorkers Battle Burgeoning Bed…" NBCNewYork.com. July 15, 2010. Accessed May 26, 2016. http://www.nbcnewyork.com/news/local/Gettin-Buggy-With-It-New-Yorkers-Battle-Bedbug-Epidemic—98447819. html.

"Six-Day War Ends–Jun 11, 1967–HISTORY.com." History. com. 2010. Accessed May 23, 2016. *http://www.history.com/ this-day-in-history/six-day-war-ends.*

Snyder, Michael. "Obama Declares War On 'Extremism' – Are You An 'Extremist' According to His Definition?" The Economic Collapse (blog) (blog), January 11, 2015. Accessed May 26, 2016. *http://theeconomiccollapseblog.com/archives/ obama-declares-war-extremism-extremist-according-definition.*

Spagat, M., A. Mack, T. Cooper, and J. Kreutz. "Estimating War Deaths: An Area of Contestation." The Journal of Conflict Resolution 53, no. 6 (December 2009): 935-36. Accessed May 22, 2016. doi:http://dx.doi.org/10.1177/0022002709346253.

Starnes, Todd. "Marine Court-martialed for Refusing to Remove Bible Verse…" Fox News. May 26, 2015. Accessed May 6, 2016. *http://www.foxnews.com/opinion/2015/05/26/marine-court-martialed-for-refusing-to-remove-bible-verse.html.*

Starnes, Todd. "Navy Chaplain Censored: 'Don't Pray in the Name of Jesus…" Fox News. April 22, 2015. Accessed May 6, 2016. *http://www.foxnews.com/opinion/2015/04/22/navy-chaplain-censored-dont-pray-in-name-jesus.html.*

Thayer and Smith. "Strong's #5604, entry for sorrow/odin." The KJV New Testament Greek Lexicon Bible Dictionary. Salem Web Network, n.d. BibleStudyTools.com. Accessed May 26,

2016. *http://www.biblestudytools.com/lexicons/greek.kjv/odin. html.* From Matthew 24:8.

UN General Assembly. "International Cooperation on Humanitarian Assistance in…" ReliefWeb. September 11, 2012. Accessed October 25, 2016. *http://reliefweb.int/report/world/international-cooperation-humanitarian-assistance-field-natural-disasters-relief-1.*

United Nations. "UN declares famine in another three areas of Somalia." UN Global Food Security. United Nations. August 3, 2011. Accessed May 22, 2016. http://www.un-foodsecurity.org/node/1177

USDA Foreign Agricultural Service. "Commodity Intelligence Reports." USDA Foreign Agricultural Service. Accessed May 21, 2016. http://www.fas.usda.gov/data/search?f[0]=field_report_type:Commodity Intelligence Reports.

USDA Foreign Agriculture Service. "Middle East: Deficient Rainfall Threatens 2009/10 Wheat Production Prospects." USDA Foreign Agricultural Service Commodity Intelligence Report. USDA. December 15, 2008. Accessed May 22, 2016. *http://www.pecad.fas.usda.gov/highlights/2008/12/mideast/*

USDA Foreign Agricultural Services. "Middle East & Central Asia: Continued Drought in 2009/10 Threatens Greater Food Grain Shortages." USDA Foreign Agricultural Services Commodity Intelligence Report. USDA. September 16, 2008. Accessed May 21, 2016. http://www.pecad.fas.usda.gov/highlights/2008/09/mideast_cenasia_drought/

USGS. "USGS FAQs: Earthquake Myths: Why are we having so many earthquakes? Has naturally occurring earthquake activity been increasing? Does this mean a big one is going to hit? OR We haven't had any earthquakes in a long time; does this mean that the pressure is building up for a big one?". USGS. Accessed May 22, 2016. https://www2.usgs.gov/faq/categories/9830/3355%20

US Dept. of Interior. "Plague in Yosemite–Yosemite National Park (U.S. National…" National Park Service. Accessed May 27, 2016. *https://www.nps.gov/yose/planyourvisit/plague.htm.*

US Dept. of State. "Foreign Terrorist Organizations–U.S. Department of State." U.S. Department of State. Accessed May 3, 2016. *http://www.state.gov/j/ct/rls/other/des/123085.htm.*

"Waco: The Inside Story, Frequently Asked Questions About Waco". Frontline, KERA tv, PBS. WGBH Educational Foundation. n.d. Accessed May 26, 2016. *http://www.pbs.org/wgbh/pages/frontline/waco/topten.html.*

Weinthall, Benjamin. "Saudi anti-Christian Sweep Prompts Calls for US Involvement". Fox News World. Fox News Network, LLC. September 14, 2014. Accessed May5, 2016. *http://www.fox-news.com/world/2014/09/14/saudi-anti-christian-sweep-prompts-calls-for-us-involvement.html.*

Wessinger, Catherine. *How the Millennium Comes Violently: From Jonestown to Heaven's Gate.* New York. Seven Bridges Press, 1999.

Wheeland, Matthew. "Brazil Struggles with Drought and Pollution as Olympics Loom Large". The Guardian. Guardian News and Media Limited. May 4, 2015. Accessed May 21, 2016. https://www.theguardian.com/sustainable-business/2015/may/04/brazil-drought-2016-olympic-games-rio-de-janiero-rio-20-climate-change.

"WGBH American Experience | PBS. Jonestown: The Life and…" PBS.org. Accessed May 26, 2016. *http://www.pbs.org/wgbh/americanexperience/films/jonestown/.*

World Health Organization. "Disease Outbreaks by Year:2010-2016." World Health Organization. WHO. n.d. Accessed May 3, 2016. http://www.who.int/csr/don/archive/year/en/.

For More Information

THIS INFORMATION WOULD BE CONSIDERED excellent information for this subject and/or related areas. It includes recommended reading as well as websites that keep updated information or have a specific article that is helpful. There is no affiliation with any of these and the author except Fear No Evil Ministries.

- FearNoEvilMinistries.org: everything there—Bible studies, prophecy and fulfillment, broadcast archive and videos, information on to-go bags, and other physical preparations.
- EMOAF.org: everything there—donation page, broadcasts, Bible classes, every tab on the menu, etc.
- Jonathan Cahn's books (*The Harbinger*, *The Mystery of the Shemitah*) and his website (HopeoftheWorld.com), where his sermons can be found.
- J. Lee Grady's "How to Be Baptized in the Holy Spirit" at CharismaMag.com of *Charisma* magazine. The article was published on March 23, 2010.
- Also by Grady is "6 Things That Block the Holy Spirit's Power" at CharismaMag.com of *Charisma* magazine. The article was published on May 21, 2015.
- "How to Speak in Tongues" at AbsoluteBibleStudy.com.
- Robert Morris's *The God I never Knew.*

About the Author

While working hard in running Fear No Evil Ministries and its website (www.fearnoevilministries.org), Amber Albrecht was told by the Lord to stop what she was doing and write an outline. This outline turned into a book guided by the Holy Spirit. In three weeks, a book was born, containing the information from the Bible that has been culminated in the work she does as a minister.

Amber sounds a warning to all, noting where in the prophetic timeline the world sits and what instructions the Bible provides for these times. She runs many social media pages associated with the ministry: Fear No Evil Ministries on Facebook, YouTube, LinkedIn, WordPress, Google+, and @fearnoevilminis on Twitter.

Fear No Evil Ministries is a global ministry spreading the gospel with a special emphasis on end-time prophecy. Amber is the founder and minister. She will continue to obey the Holy Spirit, including any future books, in doing the Lord's work as He calls. She doesn't care too much for things to concentrate on her and states she is "nothing without God."

If anyone were to want more information, they are welcome to visit any of the outlets included above.

CPSIA information can be obtained
at www.ICGtesting.com
Printed in the USA
FFOW03n1201300517
36131FF